"...an excellent book for terminal patie[nts,] pastors (who may get needed pushing [.......,] hospital personnel, ethicists, and families on the journey through grief....Very basic, offered in a caring, organized, refreshing way....The material on post-death grief, as well as ethics, offers important new insights that will stir up considerable discussion and reflection."

Chaplain Richard B. Gilbert
The Bereavement Support Group

"I found Charles Meyer's *Surviving Death: A Practical Guide to Caring for the Dying and the Bereaved* very well written, and helpful in considering the relationship between religion and medicine in caring for the dying and their families. The pastoral counsellor of the hospice here is also finding Father Meyer's work useful."

Jill A. Rhymes, M.D.
University of Chicago Medical Center

"A sensitive, helpful guide to a subject we need to think about. Charles Meyer opens new attitudes and offers specific steps to make death the natural part of life that it is."

Liz Carpenter
author of *Getting Better All the Time*

"Out of a rich experience as a hospital chaplain, Charles Meyer has written a sensitive work that will help everyone concerned with death and dying: medical practitioners, nurses, caregivers, relatives, friends, and bereaved. This work will help us to avoid the common mistakes and to cope with confidence with what most of us dread."

Reginald H. Fuller
Professor Emeritus of New Testament
Virginia Theological Seminary

"This pastoral guide by a director of pastoral care at a community hospital...offers a combination of practical and poetic advice for those who must deal with death—and that's all of us."

Catholic Standard

"Chaplain Meyer obviously possesses the credentials to illuminate the experiences of dying and assisting others to die. It is clear that he has, as a hospital chaplain, listened carefully and sensitively to many hundreds of persons who are dying themselves or who grieve for the the death of others. He has no patience with cliches, slogans, or myths, least of all from those in roles of religious leadership for some of whom these glib answers are their stock in trade.

"This is a sensible, thoughtful, balanced, and deeply biblical treatment in fresh and incisive terms."

(The Rt. Rev.) John M. Krumm
Retired Episcopal Bishop

"Chaplain Meyer begins with the premise that 'we are all dying.' By the time the reader reaches the end, it is clear that the book is unsurpassed in its concrete, step-by-step instructions on everything from walking into a patient's room, to talking with dying and bereaved individuals, and coping with the full range of emotions and behavioral demands that survivors face.

"There are many books on death and dying for professional and lay readers, but this primer will certainly surface to the top of recommended reading both for helpers and also for the dying and bereaved themselves."

Karl A. Slaikeu, Ph.D.
author of *Up From the Ashes*

Revised and Expanded

Surviving Death

·

A PRACTICAL GUIDE TO CARING FOR THE DYING & BEREAVED

CHARLES MEYER

TWENTY-THIRD PUBLICATIONS
Mystic, Connecticut

Second edition 1991

Twenty-Third Publications
185 Willow Street
P.O. Box 180
Mystic, CT 06355
(203) 536-2611

ISBN 0-89622-486-4
Library of Congress Catalog Card Number 91-65169

Preface to the Second Edition

In the two short years since this book was first published, remarkable changes have occurred in healthcare:

- The U.S. Supreme Court ruled on the case of Nancy Cruzan, a 32-year-old woman who was in a persistent vegetative state for six years when her parents began the three-year struggle to have her artificial hydration and nutrition removed. The court decided that patients have a right to refuse treatment, that states have a right to set limits to withdrawal of interventions, and that hydration and nutrition are "medical treatments" that can be withdrawn.

- Oregon proposed and debated a system of universal access to healthcare, with illnesses and conditions prioritized as to their reimbursement potential. The system has been both praised as a model for the country and condemned as limiting indigent healthcare resources still more.

- HIV infection rates have increased to 1 in 400 worldwide. Although survival time has grown from 12 to 20 months, no vaccine or cure yet exists.

- A federal patient-rights law now mandates the provision of information regarding Living Wills, Durable Powers of Attorney for Healthcare, and organ donation for all patients at time of admission.

- A proposal for active voluntary euthanasia is soon expected to be on the ballot in Washington State.

These changes are indicative of the broader changes in national healthcare—and therefore the changes in the way death is handled within our healthcare system. They are also indicative of the direction in which the whole system is moving, and have provided the basis for a revision of the original book.

Following the Cruzan decision, I received hundreds of requests for Living Wills, indicating a heightened awareness on the part of patients and families. People have come to realize, through the national headlines generated by the case and by Nancy Cruzan's subsequent death, the importance of making their wishes known about artificial interventions and extraordinary support measures.

Likewise, the Oregon plan has resulted in many other states setting up commissions to set limits on healthcare, especially since emergency rooms and trauma centers across the country are closing or reducing services. These limits and closings have affected how dying is managed and have put more of the decision making on patients and families themselves, a movement that has been echoed in the Patient Rights Bill.

Large numbers of HIV positive patients have forced the healthcare system to examine itself in terms of distribution of services, management of resources, and particularly, high-tech death. The movement for active voluntary euthanasia is a reflection of the frustration patients and families feel regarding the demand for this kind of technological dying.

Two of the new chapters are "How to Die in the 1990s" and "Hastening the Inevitable." Dying requires much greater personal preparation and assertiveness than even two years ago, and a new tool (Durable Power of Attorney for Healthcare) has been introduced to enable patients to have their interests honored and their wishes effectively carried out.

The chapter on "How to Die..." outlines the new options and explains a procedure for determining your wishes and having them carried out. The chapter on "Hastening..." explores the issue of euthanasia. Given the pressures of increasing need and decreasing access along with burgeoning biomedical technology that will keep bodies functioning for longer periods of time, that we will have to have some guidelines for active and passive "hastening" in the next five years. It is most important to begin discussion of this topic now at all levels of society to assure that fair and just limits are set as such opportunities are provided.

There are also two new chapters under the section heading of Surviving Death. The first, "Church After Death," developed out of experiences of returning to religious services following the death of a loved one. Guidelines are offered to provide a smoother and safer transition back into a worshipping community. The second chapter, "Afterlife," came about in response to several people (in one week) raising interesting and generally unanswerable questions about what happened to their loved ones after death. These questions echoed the discussions I have had with patients and families over the last twenty years, and a framework began to take shape around six areas: purpose, place, time, safety, knowledge, and future.

The addition of these four chapters, along with the revising and updating of the rest of the material, make this "handbook" an even more essential resource for dying patients, their surviving families, and all of those who care for them and will grieve with and through them. In addition, I have had people report that the information on grief and survival was helpful in other situations of loss such as divorce, separation, disability, chronic incurable illness, or job/income loss.

Thanks are due to J. Russell Hoverman, M.D., the Rev. J. Chris Hines, Chaplain Sally Barthel, Chris Morfey, Ph.D., and my wife Debi, for their perusal and suggestions regarding the new chapters. My gratitude also to the staff at Twenty-Third Publications for their helpful marketing and their willingness to publish a second edition.

Above all, my thanks are due to the patients, family, and staff at St. David's Health Care System, and those people in audiences around the country who have corroborated and added to the material from the first edition. I am honored, humbled, and gratified that *Surviving Death* has been helpful. It is my hope that this second edition will be even more so.

Austin, Texas 1991

For Parents, Mentors, and Friends

CONTENTS

SURVIVING DEATH

Introduction

There are many books on "death and dying." This is a book on survival. It developed out of my experience with dying patients and their families over the last eleven years at St. David's Hospital in Austin, Texas. In the course of that work I was asked by community organizations for help in dealing with the practical and emotional difficulties experienced by those involved with dying persons.

As I talked with these groups it quickly became clear to me that the only preparation for handling these issues came from individual family traditions. People learned how to cope with death by watching how their parents and relatives coped. There was no formal training, no open explanation of what to do or how to do it, no educational program designed to deal with personal and societal options for death, funerals, and bereavement. Indeed, my own training in college, seminary, and post-graduate school contained few or no options for the exploration of these inevitable concerns.

Because of the fear and denial associated with death, our cultural and religious institutions have relegated the responsibility for dealing with the issues surrounding death and dying to hospitals and funeral homes. But these two organizations, themselves cloaked in clinical and social mystique, have no particular monopoly on appropriate responses to dying patients, much less to bereavement. It is strange that religious institutions particularly have capitulated this responsibility to the medical establishment, which often behaves as though no one should ever die, and to the funeral home industry which, knowing everyone will, seeks to turn a profit from it.

This book addresses death and dying from many viewpoints. Dealing first with the dying process, it offers specific suggestions for what to do (and not do) with the patient and family. In exploring how we make decisions about refusing, withdrawing or withholding life support measures, we will discuss first those ethical issues which have been brought about by the increasingly technological environment in which dying occurs. The failure of the church to deal directly with these issues is examined next, along with theological misconceptions used to describe the dying process. Finally, we will assess the tasks of bereavement, including sexual interactions after the death of a loved one, and offer practical options for grieving persons as well as for those who wish to be of help to them.

This book focuses upon the caregiver; thus I hope the information and suggestions will be used by and useful to family members, nurses, physicians, Hospice and other home health workers and volunteers, as well as to high school, college and, in particular, medical school and seminary students.

I am indebted to many persons for the information presented here. Dana Joslin, R.N. and the staff of the 4 West Oncology Unit at St. David's Hospital welcomed me into their network of team care and educated me about the appropriate way to be around dying people. Phoebe Kelly, R.N., and her Intensive Care Nursery staff taught me how to respond to dying infants and their parents, as did Wanda Lary, R.N., and the Labor and Delivery nurses. Physicians John Sandbach, Dennis Welch, Harold Cain, Ruth Bain, and Don Spencer are among the many who offered varying models of bedside care with dying patients. The staff of St. David's Hospital, with their incredible ability to go out of their way to be caring and helpful, taught me about the value of the healing team—whether from housekeeping, dietary, business office, or security—in meeting the whole array of needs of the persons in our charge.

With regard to this manuscript, I am grateful to Julia Hamilton and Dana Joslin for their careful reading, thoughtful suggestions and gentle editing. Their time and effort provided clarity and encouragement, and resulted in a more complete presentation of the material.

The piece entitled "Hospice Volunteer" is included with the permission of Jean Loving, who served faithfully as a volunteer with St. David's Hospital and Hospice/Austin for many years. Her insights empathically summarize much of the didactic content of the rest of the book, and I am grateful for her viewpoint.

The three poems are by Kathyrn Morfey, a practicing Episcopalian and attorney in Southampton, England. Written in response to her eldest son's sudden accidental death (leaving a surviving daughter), the poems balance the perspective of the rest of the material. They are sensitive, thoughtful, and healing. I very much appreciate her permission to offer them here.

Most important, I am indebted to the patients and families themselves who have taught me about the incredible resilience of the human spirit. In the midst of coping with horrible debilities, excruciating pain, tortuous treatments, and embarrassing side effects, they lived and died with dignity, humor, defiance, sadness, and faith. These patients, along with the families who struggled with, and sometimes against, them in that process grieved loudly and softly with anger and acceptance, pain and relief. It is they who taught me the following lessons as we journeyed together on the road to surviving death.

I

BEING WITH THE DYING

1

How to Be With Dying Persons

We all are dying. There will come a time when each person reading these pages will not be alive. But there are some people who know they are dying before us. They have been diagnosed with a terminal illness, injured in an accident, or born with a congenital condition that guarantees a short lifespan. It is interesting that we treat these people differently than we treat each other. We treat them as though *they* are dying and *we* are not, as though death is a secret that must be guarded or a taboo that must be avoided at all costs.

Still, a part of us feels obligated to tell the secret and approach the taboo. We want to show our affection without being sad and teary. We want to ask what the person thinks and feels about dying without appearing to be intrusive or impolite. We want to share our own fears and hopes without sounding morose or unrealistic. We want to be of help but we don't know how.

There is no "right" way to behave toward a dying person. There are, however, some general principles to remember that will enhance your effectiveness and make your time together more meaningful. Because each person is different, the information presented here can offer only general guidelines. Each person can then incorporate the suggestions into his or her own particular style and method of interacting with the dying person.

Contrary to popular literature and belief, there are no "stages" of dying. The Kübler-Ross categories are helpful for observing the different behaviors likely to be seen in people who are dying. But the denial, anger, bargaining, depression, and acceptance are not always in the sequence she describes. For instance, the patient's first reaction might be anger, but it might also be bargaining or acceptance, depending on a whole list of psychological and sociological variables affecting that person. Likewise, it is not unusual for a dying patient to show depression, denial, and acceptance—all in the course of a few days, or even hours.

Thus, to simplify matters, and to avoid the already overused "stages," we will divide the time frame of dealing with a dying person into three parts: *Before, During, and After,* and will explore separately what to do—and not do—during each time.

Before   In the time preceding the death of the patient, the most important thing to remember is *be there.*

Be there consistently, as often as the patient wants you there and as frequently as your own time schedule permits. When the person is initially diagnosed, or is initially hospitalized, friends flock around for the first two weeks. They bring flowers, they offer to run errands, they stop by the hospital room with somber expressions on their faces. Wondering what to say, they try to be cheerful, offering assurances that the sick person will be just fine, and avoiding any talk of death. Then they vanish.

Naturally, people do go on with their lives when a friend or family member is initially diagnosed. Babies need to be fed, kids taken to ballet class, spouses looked after, and personal needs met. But, for the patient, a sudden change has occurred that has radically rearranged his or her outlook on life. Things that were extremely important before hearing the words "incurable," "comfort measures," or "attempt to slow the process down," are now of minor interest. Things that were taken for granted—personal projects, family relationships, friendships—are now of the highest value. The patient's life continues to go on, but with a very different perspective, and she or he may wish to share it with the very people who have suddenly disappeared.

The most common complaints, and the most poignant ones, from terminally ill patients involve isolation.

"The worst thing about this is the loneliness."

"Nobody will talk to me any more. I feel like I've done something wrong."

"Where are my friends? Where did they all go?"

"Why won't anyone listen to me talk about death?"

But being there consistently does not mean devoting every waking minute to the needs of the patient. It means continuing to go on with your own life just as everyone else does. However, unlike most everyone else, it also means continuing to maintain regular contact with the person. Whether the contact is in the form of a personal visit, a periodic phone call or letter or card, or a weekly game time or night out together (depending on the acuity of the illness), what is important is the certainty of a consistent, continuing relationship.

Most people, for whatever reason, will abandon the dying patient at some point. But to continue to stay in touch consistently with that patient reinforces the value of his or her life and indicates that you are not being scared off by the dying process. Maintaining contact on a regular basis will also, over a period of time, build the kind of relationship that will allow the patient to share with you thoughts, feelings, fears, wishes, dreams, and hopes that begin to surface as she or he comes to terms with dying. As that reality sets in, you, based on your regular contact, may be the person the patient feels most comfortable with to share ideas and opinions, or to make final plans.

It is important to remember, however, that you and your family still have obligations and duties to be maintained. You can, without feeling guilty, set limits on your involvement with the dying patient just as you would with anyone else. Everyone has realistic boundaries that preclude being at someone's beck and call every minute. Dying patients (just like the rest of us dying living folks) can understand that and appreciate the honesty. The object is to continue to go on with your life *and also* to maintain a consistent relationship of care, assistance and support with the patient throughout the entire course of the illness.

As you begin to spend time with the dying patient, from the initial diagnosis through the final breaths, be sure to *listen more than talk.* If you notice during the course of the conversation that all the words are coming from your mouth, something is wrong. Either you're not listening to what the patient is trying to say, you really don't want to hear about the pain and the death, or you're trying to cheer the patient up and avoid "unpleasant" topics, topics like the reality of dying.

It is important to *follow the patient's agenda* as you spend time in that room. Listen carefully for the clues dropped for you to follow: feelings of uncertainty as to the outcome of the illness ("I'm not sure I should bother with further treatment"); fear or apprehension about getting better ("I hope I live to see my hair grow back"); concerns about caring for the family now and later ("I wish I could be home to cook dinner tonight").

Most patients will let you know what they are willing to talk about and what they are not. It is not *required* that dying patients talk about their illness and death. Some will and some won't. What *is* required is that their friends listen to their agenda and follow it wherever it leads—from weather to whether or not they'll survive, from sports to life supports, from daily news to the latest news of their test results.

If, for whatever reason, dialogue is difficult, look around the room for clues about the person's family or friends or support system:

• Are there photographs? Who are the people? What are the relationships? Are there books lying near the bed? Ask about them.

• Are there religious materials in the room? Inquire about the person's religious background. How does he or she see God in this illness? What religious resources can be brought into the situation? Would the patient appreciate a visit from the clergy, Bible study or prayer group, or a bedside service of prayer, communion, sacrament of the sick, or baptism? Does the person wish to go to church "one last time?"

• Is the room fairly vacant and bare? What does that mean? Does it mean the patient has no friends, does not want money wasted on flowers, or does not want to be reminded that she or he is ill?

Never say to the patient: "I know how you feel." The truth is, even if you have been through a similar illness or hospitalization, neither you nor anyone else *knows* how the patient feels. Likewise, do not bring in pamphlets or articles describing miracle cures or suggesting how to deal with pain and death. Such information is extremely unhelpful, angering, and depressing for the patient.

Whatever ideas come to mind as you talk with the dying patient/family always *ask* rather than *assume*. Something that might be extremely helpful for you in the situation might not be helpful at all for the patient. Your presumption about the meaning of something the patient has said, an object you see in the room, or about what you think the patient "should" be thinking or doing may be totally inaccurate. Check out any hunches you may have directly with the patient. When in doubt, *ask*.

As you listen to the patient, help him or her to clarify whether it is "death" or "dying" that is most problematic or fearful. Since, at some level of our being, we all know that death is inevitable, most people fear the process of dying much more than death. Concerns range from uncertainty regarding pain control and loss of physical and mental functions to the effect of the patient's disability on family members, both emotionally and financially.

- "Will I die with tubes running in and out of every orifice I've got and some I didn't start out with?"
- "Will I die with loss of bowel and bladder control and be infantilized?"
- "Will I die with brain cancer causing loss of control of my words and making me say things that are terrible to my loved ones?"
- "Will I die in excruciating pain?"
- "Will I die knowing I am dying, yet unable to do anything about it?"
- "Will I die not knowing my loving spouse of many years, but knowing the nurse who has taken care of me only a few days?"

Some patients, however, will be worried about the afterlife and will want to talk with someone about religious beliefs and practices.

- "What will happen to me after I'm dead?"
- "Where will I go?"
- "Will I see my family again? My children? My wife? My parents?"
- "What happens if I don't get into heaven?"

Thus, an extremely helpful resource to the patient and family can be their relationship to a religious congregation or member of the clergy. (This can also be disastrous, as will be discussed later.)

Does the patient have a religious affiliation? Is that group willing to be of help? In some cases the congregation will supply money to help through difficult times. People from different church groups may volunteer to provide food, transportation, child-sitting service, or help with homework. They may even provide persons to stay a few hours during the day (or overnight) in the hospital room with the patient to give the family members a break from the intensity of the hospitalization and allow them to take care of the normal business details that inevitably pile up when someone is ill.

You will quickly find, however, that most people have no church, synagogue or clergy affiliation whatsoever. A recent Gallup poll found that fewer than 40 percent of Americans had any current such affiliation. In this case, many service organizations (for example, Lions, Kiwanis, Rotary, Eastern Star, Hospital Auxiliary) will provide the same service. Again, ask the patient or family about these suggestions before acting on them. It may be that they want no outside involvement at all. (In each of these situations, it is important to maintain an open attitude of offering real options that people can choose from rather than condescendingly making pointed suggestions. The task is to be sure that the needs and concerns of the patient/family are met, not that the helpers be paternalistically correct.)

Another organization that can be incredibly helpful throughout the course of the illness, the death of the patient, and the following period of bereavement with the family is Hospice. If there is a Hospice of some kind in your vicinity, check with the family or physician (most hospices require a physician's order) to see about their involvement. Sometimes the Hospice is a building, or a place patients go to die. Often, it is a program, using a variety of community resources to enable the patient to die at home. Usually a trained volunteer is assigned to the patient to be a friendly support, a listener, a companion on the final journey. It is the job of the Hospice team to help patients live those final days as fully as they are able.

Medicare patients now have the option of signing in to the Medicare Hospice program. While normal Medicare reimburses 80 percent of reasonable costs, the Medicare Hospice program reimburses at 100 percent of such costs. But the focus of care becomes *palliative only*. This means that, once the determination is made that the patient is dying, care will be aimed at comfort only, not at aggressive treatment. Usually no more CAT scans or surgery will be done, no more blood or chemotherapy will be given, tubes may be withheld or withdrawn, and antibiotics will probably not be administered in case of infection. And, of course, the patient's "code status" (resuscitative status) will switch to DNR (Do Not Resuscitate.)

Many patients and families are likely to choose this option as a reasonable alternative to aggressive, high-tech, high-cost dying. In any case, they will need caring, competent people around to help with these and other decisions.

At an appropriate time it is important to raise the issue of *death planning*. This need not be done with a morose tone or a sense of foreboding. Usually the patient will make a direct or indirect statement concerning "what will happen." At this or any other timely point, you can simply ask matter-of-factly, "Well, have you thought about any funeral plans?" Most patients are not shocked at this inquiry and, in fact, welcome the opportunity to talk about what arrangements they want and do not want.

In addition it is a good idea to check out other related areas:

• Do they have a legal, binding will?

• Do they have a durable power of attorney for healthcare in case they become incapacitated?

• Have they talked with a funeral director (and, even more importantly, with their family) and decided on the arrangements, casket of choice, type of service, hymns, and readings?

• Have they chosen someone to do the service?

• Do they want to be embalmed, viewed, cremated, buried? (All of these?)

• Have they made a decision regarding organ donations? Are they registered with The Living Bank or an Organ Procurement Agency so those wishes will be honored?

• Have they made a decision regarding extraordinary life support? Do they have a Living Will so that decision might be honored?

• Have they filled out a "Death Planning Record" indicating all of these decisions?

Finally, it is much easier for you to ask these questions of others if you have made your own plans for yourself. If you have not faced these issues, you are probably not going to feel comfortable talking about them with the patient. In fact, you may not even *hear* the patient raise the issue due to your own hesitation or fear about it. If you really want to be helpful to dying persons, take the time to make your own plans, in writing, and to discuss them with your family. Then, as issues arise, you will be much better able—and willing—to face them with the patient.

During During the actual time of the patient's dying, the most important thing you can do is, once again, *be there*. Be there as much as the patient and family want you there. A disinterested or less involved third party can often take care of the many small tasks that need to be done, such as making phone calls, cancelling or making arrangements, and organizing meals and relatives. You can also provide small comforts to ease the pain of being at the bedside, both for the patient and the family: cold cloths for the forehead of the patient, wet washcloths gently passed over the mouth or tongue to provide moisture to the dry wheezing breath, pillows carefully placed, blankets or bright quilts to maintain warmth, fans to circulate air and ease breathing, favorite music gently playing in the background.

It is hard to overstate the indelible impression made on family members in this trying time. To be there with them, providing comfort for them and their loved one is both a privilege and a gift. Your presence will be remembered always, the small tasks you performed never forgotten. But being there also means knowing what to do while there, even modeling the appropriate behavior so the other persons present will learn from you what to do.

Most people have no idea what to do around dying persons. Although many courses in death and dying deal extensively with psychological reactions, seldom do they give concrete suggestions for being at the bedside. Simply put, the most helpful things to remember are to *touch and talk.*

Tactility (the sense of touch) and hearing are the last two senses to diminish as one dies. In fact, the more the other senses fade due to coma or medication, the more sensitive and acute touch and hearing become. Contrary to the opinion of some physicians and other healthcare practitioners, it is clear that even comatose or highly sedated patients can hear and feel touch. Many times, those persons working daily with dying patients have seen responses to particular voices, individual touches and special persons entering the room. Reactions range from a sense of panic to obvious relaxation, depending on which person arrives.

In addition, the comatose or sedated person loses a sense of body boundaries, forgetting or not being able to tell where the body ends and the bed begins. Thus it is extremely important to keep touching the patient. Stroke, caress, hold, pat, or do whatever feels natural to you. You will not only help establish those body boundaries internally but also will be adding comfort and security to a very uncomfortable and insecure situation.

Talking, at first, may be more difficult. We are used to talking *with* someone, sharing information back and forth, holding a conversation. With a comatose or sedated patient who is dying, this type of interaction is obviously not possible. More desirable in this situation is to give information to the dying patient. Often this will help to orient the patient to time, place, and date. It also helps to relieve some of the fear caused by hearing voices in the room but not knowing whose they are.

Caregivers are often the worst offenders in this area. They turn patients, give baths, take temperatures and blood pressures, change i.v.'s, and give medication (even through i.v. lines) without *telling* the comatose, dying patient what they are doing. It is important to remember that these patients can hear and feel touch, may experience an internal change due to the drug or bed positioning, and may be quite fearful of that change. Thus, it is extremely important for caregivers, visitors, family, clergy, housekeeping staff, and others to explain to the patient what is being done and by whom. From fluffing a pillow to changing the sheets, dying patients must be treated as though they were fully cognizant of their surroundings on the strong possibility that they very well are.

Let the patient know who is in the room. Encourage visitors to go to the bedside (and not stay plastered against the wall, gawking) and speak to the patient. Do not *ask* the patient questions since the patient can't respond. *Tell* him or her who is touching an arm or patting a shoulder. Remind the patient of the time and date. (Dates are often important to a dying patient in terms of birthdays, anniversaries, special times of the year.) Reminisce with dying persons, telling pleasant stories or funny incidents that occurred in their lives. (It really is okay to laugh around a deathbed.) Give information about who might be coming to visit and at what time. If a beloved brother or grandchild is arriving at three in the afternoon, the dying patient may wait to die until after that arrival. If it is a less than beloved family member, the patient may decide to die sooner. Caregivers working with dying patients have witnessed both occurrences.

While in the room do not talk about the patient in the past tense, as though already deceased, or in the third person, as though not present or nonexistent. This can be very upsetting for the patient who can hear but not respond to the conversation. The dying patient may think the visitors believe that he or she is already dead and thus disregarded. Continue, instead, to treat him or her as a whole, complete, sentient person deserving of respect and acknowledgment all the way up to the time of death.

A common occurrence, and one promoted by the daytime T.V. soap operas, is demanding that dying patients do tricks for their family and visitors. The scenario usually involves the tearful son or daughter coming in at the last minute from out of town, frantically rushing up to the bedside of the comatose patient and demanding in loud, sobbing tones: "Momma! If you can *hear* me, *squeeze* my hand!" Or ..."*blink* an eye!" Or "...*wiggle* a toe!" Or "...*nod* your head!"

Remember that the patient is using every ounce of energy just to force air in and out of gurgling lungs and so cannot begin to perform these acts to please and reassure the visitor. Imagine yourself in the patient's position: you can hear the request and you very much want somehow to let this loved one know that you do hear, and understand that you are still alive and listening to their words. And yet it is all you can do to breathe or to remember to breathe, to gasp at times for air, to muster your strength to suck in one more shallow breath. You want desperately to "squeeze...blink...wiggle ...or nod" and you just *can't* do it. Imagine how frustrating that would be for you and how disappointed you would feel that you had failed your loved one's last request.

Dying patients have enough to worry about and plenty of hard work to do without being asked to perform and respond in their final moments. Give them information, treat them with the dignity they deserve, and comfort them with touch and talk.

Throughout the length of the illness, and especially during the hours or minutes immediately preceding death, arrangements need to be made for the patient and family member, friend, spouse, or significant other to have *time alone*. Friends and family members frequently forget that a couple has spent twenty, thirty, or fifty years together and might like some personal, or even intimate moments to hold, to touch, to say things one last time before they part. The same need is often present for younger patients and their friends, as well as for infants and parents. Be sensitive to this need for time alone and offer to arrange for it.

Depending upon the religious belief system of the patient, *prayer* can be a meaningful way to comfort and support someone during the dying process. If the patient is lucid and responsive, first *ask* what she or he would like to pray about. Do not assume that you know what's important to the patient at that time.

A woman going in for a Hickman Catheter placement was asked if she wanted to have a prayer. When asked what she wanted to pray about, she replied, "my divorce," a subject she had not mentioned in the entire interview up to that time. Asking patients what they want to pray about is a powerful way to get at the most pressing concerns on their mind at that time.

Next, pay close attention to what is said, as you may be asked to offer it up in prayer. Then ask if the person would like to start or would prefer for you to begin. Gather others in the room around the bedside, touch the patient, tell the patient (if comatose) what you are doing together, and invite his or her participation with you. Keep it relatively short and also invite the persons gathered around the bed to offer their prayers or comments silently or aloud.

Many things may happen at the time of death. (See Appendix.) Usually the patient will wind down slowly, breathing ever more shallowly until the breath finally ceases. Facial contortions, muscle jerks, and skin color changes are not uncommon. Occasionally the contents of the lungs or stomach may be aspirated or vomited up, and loss of bladder and bowel control will result in urine and feces being excreted. Most of the time the death will be quiet and peaceful, aided and supported by all of the things you and others have done by being present there.

After Following the death, whether immediately or long term, again the most important thing to remember is *be there.* Be attentive without being obtrusive. Be available to hold the survivors as they express their sorrow in the room. Escort them to a waiting area while the nurses remove tubes and prepare the body to be picked up. Help them make the phone call to the funeral home and to begin to make funeral and other arrangements for the coming few days of organized confusion. Offer to help pack up the room for or with them and help them remember to check the bedside table, closet, window sill, and under the bed for personal belongings.

While waiting for the funeral home, ask if you can help with phone calls or food arrangements, gently reminding survivors that they will need to eat to keep up their own strength in the coming days. Ask what they are tentatively planning to do for the next twenty-four hours. This question begins the process of thinking about the future and moving slowly beyond the painful present.

When the funeral home attendant arrives and people have said their goodbyes, there is frequently a reluctance on the part of the family to leave the hospital. It is very difficult, sad, and lonely to leave carrying the remnants of the illness and of the relationship in plastic bags.

Support the family in whatever makes them feel best. There is no need for them to hurry to leave the hospital. They can leave when they feel comfortable or when they gather the strength to do so. Be sure to escort them from the room to the car. The longest walk in the world is from the empty hospital room where a loved one has died to the car that is now filled only with fading flowers and plastic bags of memories.

Because many survivors become disoriented following a death, it is wise to assess their ability to drive. Offer to call a cab, to drive them home, or to follow them in your car if a family member or friend is not available to do so. Walk the survivor(s) into the empty house for the first time, or arrange for someone to be there when they arrive, to help them deal with the feelings and thoughts that will inevitably surface.

While the information here has focused primarily on hospitalized patients, the same suggestions apply when the patient is dying at home. The involvement of Hospice, the rising cost of (and lower reimbursement for) inpatient care, and the increasing availability of supportive home care services have combined to enable more and more persons to be at home for the final days of their lives. (See Chapter 4.)

Patients frequently want to die amidst the familiar surroundings of their own bedroom or den, maintaining closer contact with neighbors and friends, and having favorite pets at their side. Families, fearing they will be unable to adequately care for their loved one, or thinking they will always see the person dead in that room, usually want the patient to die in the emotionally neutral territory of the hospital. Thus, when the decision is made to die at home, both patient and family will need the constant support and encouragement of friends.

When the patient does die in the home, care must be taken to avoid the extremely unpleasant, though frequent, occurrence of having the EMS (Emergency Medical Services) arrive with lights, sirens, police cars, and fire trucks. In addition, EMS personnel will usually feel obligated to attempt to resuscitate the person, even though the person has been dead for some time.

Proper arrangements often can be made by first calling the physician and then notifying the funeral home. Since laws and practices vary widely from state to state, it is important for the family to check with the physician or Hospice program ahead of time to know how to avoid this potentially traumatizing scene for the family at the moment of death.

Whether the death occurs at home or in the hospital, as time goes by remember to *be there* by periodically checking in with the survivor. Friends, neighbors, and other family members will flock around (just as they did during the initial diagnosis) for about two weeks following the funeral. Then, as is to be expected, they leave and go on with their lives. You may be the *only* person who calls one month, three months, six months, or a year later *on the date of the death* to express your concern and to offer to stop by for coffee, take the person to lunch, and be available to listen. You may be the *only* person who is not afraid to call on holidays, birthdays, anniversaries, or other special times to show your support and risk having the person cry with you. You may be the *only* person who checks in periodically and is willing to hear the pain told and relived again and again.

As you maintain contact and continue to hear the survivor's struggle with grief, *do not demand* that the survivor hurry up and "get over it." Many persons, due to their own discomfort with death and sad feelings, will push the survivor to "get on with life" and "stop thinking about the past." They will say and do insensitive things, encouraging the grieving person to get rid of personal mementos of the deceased and to take on new commitments, relationships, and obligations so as to ignore the grief and accept the future.

Once again, you may be the *only* person who is not pushing the survivor to change, to date, to go out with people, to throw out clothes or take down pictures, to move and change jobs. You may be the *only* person who is willing to listen to the tears and loneliness, and even encourage their expression, two or three years after the event, with the same empathy you offered on the day of the death.

NEONATAL DEATH

Death of an infant at birth or shortly thereafter is thought by many people to be the most difficult of losses to handle. In addition to the helplessness and innocence that make the death seem unfair, the abrupt ending of a life not yet begun is, for some people, more tragic than death at the conclusion of years of relationships. The death of an adult is the death of a memory. The death of a child is the death of a dream.

But others express relief that the infant did not live or survive very long. They find it easier to handle the death now than months or even years later. In any case, neonatal death involves some special procedures in addition to the general care of the patient and family described above.

Care relating to the infant and parents follows the same guidelines as with adults: be there, touch and talk, ask rather than assume, listen more than you talk, and offer to be available for other family members. In addition, a hospital staff member (nurse, chaplain, social worker) will offer some options to the parents that will require discussion and support.

If possible, shortly before the time of death, in the Intensive Care Nursery where the infant is attached to artificial support, or in the delivery room where the stillborn is about to be delivered, the parents will be prepared by a staff member for some of the decisions facing them after the death has occurred. They will need to begin thinking about funeral arrangements, religious services, and cremation or burial, depending on the size and weight of the infant or fetus. (Many states set the gestational limit at 20 weeks; if below that number the fetus may be disposed of as tissue, above 20 weeks it must have some legal disposition.) Even if the fetus is under the weight or gestational limit legally requiring such services, the family can still have a funeral and burial if they wish.

Though it may sound macabre to those who have never witnessed such an occasion, the couple also will be offered the opportunity to see and hold the dead infant. After the woman recovers from the anesthesia, or rests from the birthing process, she and the father will be asked, and even encouraged, to see the baby. Although the choice is up to the parents, it is helpful to explain that "...though this is a tragic, difficult time for you, I can tell you that people have come back six months later to say how meaningful the time was."

A staff member (frequently from Pastoral Care) will bring the infant into the room, wrapped in a blanket, and place it in the mothers's arms. The parents (and whomever else they want in the room—grandparents, children, friends) are encouraged to touch and hold the baby for as long as they wish. One couple with premature twins expressed the meaning of spending time with the dead babies in this way: "I just wanted to get to know them before I had to give them up."

In the case of an anomalous baby with some physiological defect, the healthy, fully formed parts of the child will be pointed out in contrast to the deformity. Even with a deformed baby, the reality of touching and looking is almost never as bad as it is in the mind and imagination of the parents.

Sometimes the physician or family will request an autopsy to attempt to determine the cause of the anomaly. While many families recoil at the thought of "cutting on our child," others will permit the procedure to relieve their concern about future children. A common guideline is the "six month rule:" "If you can project yourself six months into the future and think you will be satisfied with understanding the cause of the child's death, then you probably do not need to do the autopsy. If you can imagine that in six months you will look back and wonder what happened, then you probably do need to have it done."

Usually the couple also will be asked if they want the baby baptized. For persons with a sacramental religious tradition (Roman Catholic, Episcopalian, Lutheran, Methodist) this event may be very important. It symbolizes the welcoming of the baby into the religious community and, by its performance, recognizes the baby as a fully human member of the church and of that particular family. In situations where the fetus is under the gestational age or weight limit and is stillborn, no birth or death certificate is issued to the parents and the baptismal certificate may be the only document that indicates they actually had a baby. Such a remembrance is very important to help fill some of the emptiness that results in the loss of a child at birth.

Unfortunately, many clergy will not baptize a dead baby. They cite theological arguments against the practice for the child and ignore the extremely positive *pastoral* support it provides for the family. Theological arguments can also be made that baptism is the welcoming initiation of the infant into the *larger church*, the whole *Communion of Saints*, consisting of the entire "cloud of witnesses," past and present, those living and dead. Most hospital chaplains, therefore, will perform this service for the family, having had experience with the relief, acceptance, and healing it provides for parents at the time of the death as well as months later.

Naming the child is a very powerful and tender event. It can be done in the context of baptism or in a secular manner for persons not of those religious traditions, by simply giving the child a name and referring to him or her by that name. In either case, the procedure gives the family someone to mourn and remember. It also has the effect of making the baby a person in the present. Many times a mother initially will refuse to name the child. She refuses to hold, look at, or acknowledge his or her presence. But once we have baptized or named the infant, the wall crumbles and she reaches out and calls her child by name, looks at and holds the child, and weeps as her family does the same.

In addition to the above options, most Intensive Care Nurseries or Labor and Delivery Units will take pictures of the infant for the parents. Usually these will be held by Pastoral Care or Social Services and given to the parents when and if they want them. Once again, the pictures, time spent with the dead infant, and perhaps a baptism or naming ceremony, all reinforce for the grieving couple the reality of the birth and death, and help to fill the emptiness they feel at this time, and in the future.

Often, parents, relatives, or well-meaning friends of the couple will want to rush to the house and dismantle the nursery, making sure the room is returned to its former state, with the baby clothes carefully packed away, before the mother comes home. This mistake, however, will only lead to a feeling of even greater emptiness and disappointment. While it is extremely painful for the couple to return to the room they had set up to receive the newborn, it is a realistic and meaningful part of the grieving process for them to take things down and put them away together. As will all other well-meant offerings, remember to *ask* what the wishes of the couple are, and then honor those wishes.

Finally, just as with adult deaths, *be there* after the event to support and listen to the pain as the days, months, and even years pass. One of the major common occurrences following the death of an infant is marital difficulty between the parents, frequently leading to separation or divorce. You may be the *one* person who is willing to hear and acknowledge the pain of both parents, separately expressed, support both in their loss, and possibly recommend counseling to work out the anger, resentment or disappointment stirred up by the death.

The death of an infant is indeed a tragic and difficult loss. It can be made more tolerable with the help of those persons who are willing to accept and encourage the distraught and often disbelieving parents in their grief.

Reading and following the above guidelines for *Before, During,* and *After* death will be helpful in dealing with dying patients and their families. But there is another factor which, if not taken seriously, will prohibit you from approaching the bedside with a willingness to listen, to hear and to discuss the issues of death and dying. That factor is your own fear or comfort with your *own* death.

Larry Bugen, Ph.D., a therapist and educator in private practice in Austin, Texas, has written and lectured extensively on loss and grief and has carefully observed reactions to death in himself and others. During a class on "Death and Dying" he had arranged to have as a guest speaker a woman who was terminally ill. Before she came into the room, he pre-tested the class, asking the students a list of questions that would indicate their comfort level with their own deaths. The woman then joined the class, spoke of her illness and impending death, and her feelings about dying. After she left, Dr. Bugen post-tested the class, asking questions that would elicit how well the students thought the woman was coping with her situation.

Not surprisingly, after comparing the two sets of responses, Dr. Bugen found that the students who saw themselves as having a very difficult time talking or thinking about their own deaths saw the woman as coping very poorly with her death. The students who reported a level of relative comfort in discussing or planning for their own deaths thought the woman was handling her death quite appropriately and with courage.

The implication here is obvious. If you *seriously* want to be of help to dying patients and their families, take the time to come to terms with your *own* death. Ask yourself the same series of questions listed in the *Before* section; then carry them out. Make a will. Plan your funeral arrangements. Compose a healthcare durable power of attorney and sign a Living Will. Talk with your family or significant others about your plans and wishes.

If you do *not* do these things yourself, you are very likely to avoid the subject with dying patients and possibly not even *hear* them cautiously bring up their concerns. When you have made your plans, faced the fearful issue of your own demise, and explored with someone close to you the feelings of anger, disappointment, hope or surprise about your own death, you will be more comfortable, open, and effective in being with others who are dying. And you also will have begun your own process of surviving the inevitable deaths of people you love.

II

ETHICS AND DEATH

2

Death Myths

As everyone knows, medical decision making in the area of withholding, refusing, or withdrawing life support has become increasingly complex and difficult. New technology has had the most obvious impact on these dilemmas as patients, families, and physicians are offered more and ever newer diagnostic and life prolonging equipment.

• CAT scanners have been supplanted by Magnetic Resonance Imagery (MRI) machines which use no radioactive materials and produce incredibly clear (computer assisted) pictures. They will soon be able to do blood chemistry and enzyme analysis without venipuncture (drawing blood).

• New neonatal respirators push air into the undeveloped lungs of infants with greater impact, forcing more oxygen exchange and enabling even more and smaller premature babies to stay alive longer.

• Laser technology will soon be used in cardiology to replace the current "balloon" technique of destroying plaque inside clogged arteries, virtually opening them entirely.

While technology has increased our options for treatment (or non-treatment) in both crisis and long term illnesses, it is usually not the determining factor in making such decisions. Rather, there exists a set of subtle and extremely powerful internal presuppositions which inform and direct our choices regarding withdrawing, withholding, or refusing life support. It is necessary to examine these deep seated, culturally reinforced death myths in order to more openly and realistically evaluate the appropriate options for and with dying patients and their families.

Whether based on medical tradition, social obligation, or religious teaching, the death myths influencing which treatment decisions we make are indelibly embedded within our collective psyche. They flash through our minds when the doctor tells us the patient's condition is poor. They are the screens through which we hear the diagnosis of serious illness. They are the standards against which we weigh our response to the terminal prognosis. They are not "myths" in the traditional sense of beliefs which represent symbolic truth, but are myths in the usual, popular sense of ideas which obscure the truth, or even serve to perpetuate falsehoods.

The death myths most prominent in our culture are as follows:

1. *"Only old people die."* Conversely stated, this means that "Young people should not die." Neither assumption is true. The mortality information from most hospitals shows that nearly equal (and, as AIDS patients become more prominent, increasingly greater) numbers of people under age 65 die, especially in the 0 to 10 category.

It is agism at its worst to think that an old person has "lived his or her life" and therefore is more accepting or more deserving of death than a younger, 20- to 40-year-old counterpart. In fact, it is entirely possible for the situation to be quite the reverse; the aged person may be more vital and have more to live for than the youth.

Belief in this myth can result in young persons undergoing extraordinary efforts from chemotherapy to intubation *just because* they are young, or old persons prematurely denying further treatment *just because* they are old. The myth also serves to reinforce our own wish for a long life, and to defend against our fear of our own death coming "prematurely."

The truth is, whether we like it or not, people of all ages die. Death is no respecter of age. There is no guarantee of lifespan given with conception. Each death is sad, tragic, acceptable or a relief based on the life of the person, the quality of that life, and the kinds of relationships that person has had. Each dying situation, therefore, where a decision must be made to withhold or withdraw artificial intervention, needs to be evaluated on those criteria, not on a myth about age that presumes that it is "okay" for old (but not young) persons to die, perhaps intimating that the elderly want to die or even ought to die.

2. *"Medicine can cure everything."* Even in the face of long term illness when the patient is finally about to die, panicked family members frequently ask "Can't you *do* something?" The panic and the request (or demand) reflect a strong belief in this country that medicine can find and cure all illness and physicians are or should be omniscient.

The media to the contrary, most physicians, and other health care professionals, do not act to reinforce this image. (They know better.) Rather, the myth persists because it is what people very much want to believe. As another denial of the inevitability of illness or death it is we ourselves who want to believe that drugs, medical technology, and their physician purveyors can prevent or cure the effects of disease, self inflicted injury (smoking, diet, lifestyle), and aging.

But it is also true that the medical community has frequently oversold the efficacy or advisability of a particular technical or therapeutic breakthrough. The artificial heart was an example of such a media event. Regardless of the availability, advisability, and ruinous financial cost of this device, the heart was proffered as another example of technology's ability to cheat death, and the myth was reinforced. Similar claims are being made for transplantation of fetal brain tissue and for the use of other exotic, experimental, and expensive treatments that often later prove to be equally or less effective than the previous treatment.

It is more honest to be straight with patients and ourselves about the limits of tests, treatments, medications, and tentative prognoses. Not to do so is to embrace this myth of medicine and to end up feeling angry, disappointed, guilty, and resentful.

Medicine cannot cure everything. Death is a normal bodily function. It is not optional for the human race.

3. *"Life is always the highest value."* The initial presumption in nearly any accident or illness is always in favor of preserving life. But once the patient is stabilized and the prognosis is clear, considerations other than the priority of "life" come into effect. It is at this point that the meaning and quality of life *as the patient experiences them* are of the highest value in making the hard decisions of treatment and life support.

The easy temptation is to presume the patient either believes or ought to believe this myth, especially if the physician does. To presume that life is of the highest value supports our own refusal to see death as an acceptable outcome for the patient, and for ourselves. Fortunately, however, families and patients are increasingly moving toward the "meaning and quality" standard of judgment for discontinuing treatment. They seem to understand that life is more than breathing, living is more than subsisting, and presence with us means more than physically being there.

4. *"Money should not be a consideration."* This myth is supported by those who believe it is crass and insensitive to give the cost of treatment any weight in medical decision making. In our "bottom line" oriented culture we see the consideration of money to somehow diminish the image of the person. We rightly reject placing a monetary value on a person's life. We emotionally recoil at the prospect of finances determining treatment, preferring to spend "whatever is necessary" to save the life of our loved one.

But what of the young couple whose baby is dying yet can be kept alive a few more hours or days in our technologically equipped Intensive Care Nurseries? Or the elderly woman maintained by a respirator in ICU whose husband is barely subsisting on Social Security? And what of the use of resources devoted to these dying patients (not just for comfort but for continuing active treatment that is much more than palliative) that could be used for taking care of other, curable patients, for research, or for reducing hospital costs for everyone?

The honest, if uncomfortable, truth is that money is *already* a consideration in medical decision making and it will continue to play an even greater role as healthcare rationing becomes a reality in the United States. Given a limited amount of resources and a virtually unlimited demand, it is reasonable to conclude that financial concerns are and will be a part of the process of deciding to withhold or withdraw treatment. (See Chapter 4.)

As many European countries have done, the United States has begun to experiment with healthcare rationing. In Great Britain, if a person over the age of 55 comes to a hospital with cardiac arrest, she or he can be treated and kept comfortable, but open heart surgery will not be done; neither will renal dialysis. In Sweden the age cut off is 50.

Similarly, as mentioned earlier, if patients are on Medicare (where hospital bills are reimbursed at 80 percent of reasonable cost) and have less than six months to live, they can switch into the Medicare/ Hospice track. Bills will then be reimbursed at 100 percent of reasonable cost, but the patient agrees to go ahead and die.

And it is not unreasonable, in the case of dying patients, to suggest that the focus of care switch from curative (an unrealistic goal) to palliative. Concentrating on pain control, dignity, safety, comfort, and quality of remaining life, the patient will usually no longer receive further chemotherapy, blood transfusions, CAT scans, or antibiotics for infections. Pain is palliated, patient comfort is the highest goal, and costs of expensive and extraordinary technology and treatments are dramatically reduced.

As our entire healthcare system undergoes more changes in the coming years, more areas of rationing will inevitably appear. In the meantime, it can be argued that, sensitively done, consideration of the family's or patient's financial situation is a *very* caring gesture, as is weighing the effect of treatment on the cost of healthcare to the entire community, indeed to the nation. As the percent of GNP spent on healthcare jumps from the current 12 percent to as much as 15 percent by 1995 (approaching 20 by the year 2000), financial considerations will become even more important as patients weigh their treatment options.

5. *"Death is evil. Death means failure."* While the church is largely responsible for promoting the first of these, the medical/ healthcare profession is responsible for the persistence of the second.

Many people, desperately attempting to make some kind of logical sense out of their illness, have been told by their religious community that good is always rewarded and evil is always punished. They then extrapolate that good is always a reward and evil is always a punishment. They are sick or dying, therefore they must have done something bad and incurred the punishment of a wrathful God.

In fact death is not evil; neither is it intrinsically good. Sickness and death are *amoral* occurrences. They have nothing to do with good/bad, right/wrong, punishment/reward. We get sick. We die. As one doctor said: Welcome to Earth; the death rate here is 100%. One out of one dies."

The only thing "good" or "bad" about death is the manner in which one responds to it. Death, like any other amoral occurrence (birth, accident, marriage, divorce, trauma) is merely an occasion for good or evil to become manifest. That manifestation is shown in our response to the event, not in the event itself.

Likewise death has nothing to do with failure. Assuming one has done everything necessary (not possible, but necessary) and the patient's condition is said to be "incompatible with life," it is understandable that the person dies. The death has nothing to do with the ability of the physician or nursing staff. "Success" and "failure" are value judgments that reveal the bias of the training of health-care staff (using military terminology—triage, fight, battle, win/lose, bravery).

Such judgments have no meaning when applied to the event of the death, which is *amoral*. In fact, it seems the height of arrogance to assume that we (patient, family or physician) have "failed" when a natural process (death) has followed its normal route. To support this myth is the same as saying hurricane or earthquake victims "failed" to stop the hurricane or earthquake.

All this is not to imply that death is not often sad, angering, relieving, unfair, or crushing. It is all this and more in feeling terms. The problem arises in treating death as though it should not happen, denying it as a logical, acceptable, and sometimes desirable possibility for the outcome of the patient's illness.

Death might more easily be tolerated by all of us if we saw it as a form of *healing*. Death as healing transposes its symbolic meaning from that of evil enemy to that of an acceptable, and at times even welcomed, alternative.

6. *"Where there's life there's hope."* This myth, though frequently cited when making treatment decisions, is patently untrue. Where there's life there is quite often the opposite of hope: There is agony, fear, excruciating pain, anger, frustration, loneliness, and despair. The sentiment really expressed here is that where there is biological

activity (whether mechanically assisted or otherwise), there is reason for optimism that the person may recover, even against all odds.

The questions to be asked of this myth are: "What is life?" and "What is hope?" Is life merely the activity of air being forced into stiffening lungs, or blood being pumped inside a human cavity? Is it biological activity mechanically produced or substantially supported? Again the quality of life standard (as judged by the patient if competent or by the patient's significant others if incompetent) comes into consideration. Increasing numbers of people believe that life is not life if there is no quality of relating, quality of experiencing and enjoying, quality of being. Life, for them, means much more than the rather shallow definition of longevity.

"Hope," also, is quite different from "optimism." Optimism demands the patient get well (not just better) and return to the former state of health. Nothing less is desirable or acceptable. The meaning of hope, on the other hand, was expressed by a cancer patient who commented: "It's okay with me if I live and it's okay with me if I die. Because either place I'm loved." Hope implies that death is as acceptable an outcome to one's condition as life. Hope embraces and affirms both life and death as parts of a greater whole of existence. Hope sees life not as a problem to be solved but as a mystery to be lived, and death as a part of that mystery.

7. *"Suffering is redemptive."* Believe it or not, some people (patients, families, physicians and nurses), will refuse pain medication, withhold palliative measures to increase comfort, or deny the obvious existence of pain because they see the suffering as cleansing, deserved, or redemptive. Followers of this myth, based on a conservative theological or philosophical tradition, conquer their own helplessness in the face of illness and death by assuming that discomfort and pain are spiritually or psychologically helpful to the patient.

Of course it is sometimes true that suffering can be an occasion for redemption, for the healing of memories, relationships, hurts, fears, or guilts. Pain and illness often are the precipitators of change in behavior or perspective on the person's lifestyle. But suffering is also quite often the occasion for unquenchable bitterness, debilitating despair, collapse of faith and disintegration of personhood.

Once again, in our attempts to make sense of an illness we want to believe there is some purpose, some plan, some reason for the horrible suffering we or our loved ones are enduring. Once again, the truth is that suffering is as amoral as the virus, bacteria, or systemic condition that is its cause.

But redemption or collapse are *responses* to the pain and discomfort. These individual and varied responses depend largely on the personality and belief system of the patient, and the quality of interactions between the patient and loved ones, not on the condition or amount of suffering the patient experiences.

8. *"Once you start something, you can't stop it."* Physicians, nurses, and technicians are the most common purveyors of this myth. It is also reflected in the common knowledge bank of misinformation about healthcare on the part of families and patients. Usually stated in relation to respirators, artificial hydration and nutrition, or heart pumps, it represents the reluctance to withdraw treatment, based on the premise that it is morally better (and easier) not to start a procedure than it is to withdraw or discontinue one. By not starting a treatment, death is seen to be passively allowed; when treatment is stopped, death is thought to be "caused" by the deletion of "life-sustaining" interventions.

The truth is that any treatment may be withdrawn at any time if and when that treatment is futile or harmful. There will be some instances when it will be apparent that such treatments are futile and should not be begun. In other cases, there will be a modicum of doubt, and treatment will be started to see if in fact it is futile, in which case it should—as with any other futile or inappropriate or harmful treatment—be stopped. (See Chapter 5.)

9. *"Pulling the plug is suicide or murder."* Many people refuse to make a decision to withdraw hydration, nutrition, or respiratory maintenance because they believe such an act constitutes murder. Likewise, to designate a personal directive such as a Living Will may seem tantamount to suicide. The underlying presupposition is that it is improper to take any control over one's own death. To do so is seen to usurp the power and prerogative of an all-controlling God.

In fact, not to decide is to decide. Not to make a Living Will, designate a surrogate decision maker, or withdraw artificial intervention systems is to decide to abdicate responsibility. It is to relegate the burden of decision making to someone (physician, hospital, committee, court) far less qualified to make it, and refuse to accept our ability and responsibility as "co-creators with God" to share in the rational determination of our destiny.

One could just as easily argue that not to pull the plug or make a Living Will designation is to stand in the way of Nature, God, and the normal procession of life to death.

A major theological task for the church is to re-examine its beliefs regarding suicide, assisted suicide, active and passive euthanasia, to adjust to modern technological developments, and to enable individuals to exercise options that, heretofore, were unacceptable.

10. *"To die of dehydration or starvation in a healthcare setting is inhumane, cruel, and immoral."* When many people think of food and drink, they imagine sitting down at a table with steaming dishes and good friends. But that image of wholesome food staring invitingly at us (and we, hungrily, back at it) is vastly different from the reality of the dying patient, or even the vegetative non-dying patient, who is maintained by artificial nutrition and artificial hydration.

Instead, picture blue humming boxes sucking high calorie pastel liquid from bags and bottles and forcing it through clear plastic tubing into the patient's nose or directly into the stomach or intestine. This artificial intervention is ethically and legally parallel to the use of a respirator that artificially pumps air in and out of failing lungs.

In addition, it is important to realize that the natural process of death is totally subverted by our demand that loved ones die in the midst of high-tech drama. In fact, before the technological armamentarium included such things as respirators, i.v. pumps, or the Thumper (mechanically-conducted CPR) patients usually went home to die, assisted only by drugs to relieve the pain. Anorexia (lack or loss of appetite) first set in, followed closely by dehydration and malnutrition.

Dehydration and malnutrition cause azotemia, (a condition in which) the body's waste nitrogen products become elevated in the blood, and these products, acting as a natural sedative, diminish a patient's awareness and elevate the pain threshold.

Appetite decreases, alertness diminishes, and the obtunded patient (one whose senses are dulled) dies; the stuporous state suffices to free the patient of pain.

The technological imperative to have patients die in electrolyte balance and well-hydrated is a grave disservice. It serves only to ward off the sedative effect of the azotemia. The result not only increases pain perception, but also adds to the mental agony of the patient who is kept alert enough to appreciate his or her situation. (Abrams, "Withholding Treatment When Death Is Not Imminent," 42 *Geriatrics* 77, 84, No. 5, May 1987)

For increasing numbers of people, to die of dehydration or starvation while being kept comfortable with the large array of palliative drugs available is far preferable and much more humane than the prolonged dying by incessant medical intervention that is demanded of patients by misinformed relatives and practitioners, acting on outdated and ineffectual death myths.

It is clear that these death myths at one time served a proper and meaningful role in medical decision making. It is equally clear that they can no longer serve that same role. As a part of the standard cultural presuppositions about life, death, and medicine, these myths stood to call all the available medical resources to the service of life at any cost. But current technology has changed the perspective about and meaning of the concepts of life, death, and medicine. As these concepts are revised in light of even newer treatment options, we will need to develop a different, more flexible set of "death myths" to guide our treatment decisions. (Some of these guidelines are presented in the next chapter.)

It is important to examine and acknowledge how much we rely on these outdated presuppositions. Only then will they not become impediments to caring, meaningful decision making regarding the treatment and life support choices offered to our loved ones—and to ourselves.

3

Pulling the Plug: How Do We Decide?

The Lone Ranger and Tonto were out in the middle of the prairie surrounded by thousands of Indians. From their hiding place behind the rocks they could see Apaches to the North, Sioux to the South, Cherokee to the East, and Kiowa to the West. The supply of silver bullets was dwindling. It was clear that the end was near. The Lone Ranger turned to Tonto and said: "Well, old faithful companion, old Kemosabe, old friend, we've been down a lot of dusty trails together. But it looks like we won't make it out of this one alive." Tonto then looked over at The Lone Ranger and replied with a smile, "What you mean, 'we,' White Man?"

In considering the withdrawal or withholding of life support, it is well to remember that the patient is usually in the Lone Ranger's position, while we are in the rather enviable position of being Tonto. It is also well to remember that we Tontos will one day be in the Masked Man's situation ourselves, so our decisions must be carefully made, for future reference.

The answer to the question "How do we decide?" and the perspective from which it is approached can vary with who *we* are. On the one hand "we" are the caregivers, the family, close friends, physicians, nurses, clergy, social workers, attorneys, and other healthcare professionals involved with the dying patient. But it is equally important to realize that (with Tonto) "we" are also the dying, and to use that realization to empathize more closely with the person lying before us. Had Tonto understood this fact, he would not have smiled so broadly as he withdrew the Lone Ranger's life support.

Life support decisions are made in two basic contexts:

1. crisis situations
2. non-crisis, longer term spans of time

While some of the considerations and guidelines for decision making in both situations overlap, it is important to deal with the contexts separately, as different dynamics are present in each.

CRISIS SITUATIONS

• Your spouse of twenty-eight years has been brought into the Emergency Department with a stroke and is paralyzed on the left side. He never wanted to be on a respirator but requires one now to keep breathing. His blood pressure is falling but can be maintained with drugs.

• Your newborn infant has severe congenital anomalies. She can be kept alive for days or even a few weeks in the Intensive Care Nursery at $1200 per day. Then she will eventually die.

• Your 86-year-old father has had a massive heart attack. He is on a respirator in the Intensive Care Unit, and his physician recommends immediate open heart surgery before he arrests again.

Deciding what to do and how to do it in crisis situations such as these can be extremely problematic. The pressures of time, emotionalism, and uncertainty of outcome weigh heavily on those who must sign consent forms and act in the patient's stead. To provide some order to this chaos, the following guidelines may be helpful.

1. Get the best information available. It is important to know how many Indians are *really* out there and how many silver bullets are *really* left. Talk to the physician, and listen when he or she answers you. Many families complain that their physician did not tell them everything, when in fact they themselves did not want to hear and so did not listen.

Ask as many questions as you need to ask. Write your questions down while waiting for test results and don't let the physician go until you get answers. Remember that the physician (like any other consultant you might hire) works for you, and you have a right to know all of the information gathered. You are also free to get a second opinion, or even a third given the constraints of time. Many physicians will request or encourage another opinion anyway. Having heard their best experienced conclusions as to diagnosis and prognosis, the decision regarding treatment and life support is up to you.

2. *Aim for a balance.* If the patient is competent (awake and able to converse), consider first what she or he wants done. If the patient is incompetent it will be up to you (individually or in consultation with other family and friends) to determine what you think he or she would want done. In nearly every situation the wishes of the patient should be given priority and honored wherever possible.

Next, balance off the wants and needs of the patient with those of the family. It is vital that no unilateral decisions be made. Both the desires of the patient and the desires of the family or significant other need to be considered and a consensus carefully reached. Sometimes it is appropriate to consider the needs of the larger community as well: for example, will this expenditure of healthcare (respirator, neonatal or ICU bed space, dialysis, heart surgery) limit the available resources for less catastrophically ill patients? What is our ethical consensus, if any, on the provision of lifetime care for severely disabled persons?

Consider the emotional issues of the past, present and future. How has this person dealt with decisions in the past? What is this person feeling about the present dilemma? What will be the emotional fallout for the patient (assuming treatment and survival) or for the family (assuming withdrawal of treatment and death) in the future? Imagine yourself six months from now. How will you feel about this decision then?

3. *Seek disinterest and clarity.* People in crisis need someone to help who is disinterested but not uninterested, someone who will help seek clarity about the issues without the distortion of personal involvement. If you are the person in crisis, seek out someone (pas-

toral care, social services, patient representative) who will assist in this way. If you are the helper to someone else, know when to make a referral if the issue hits too close to home for you.

Remember that time is not always of the essence. Usually you need not feel pressured into instant decision making (unlike the dramas portrayed on the soaps). Take the time you need to defuse the "crisis orientation" of the decision and get some help either from friends or from professionals at the hospital.

4. Ethic of love. Ethic of need. Two major guidelines that are helpful in crisis decision making are the those of "love" and "need." Jesus' suggestion that we love our neighbor as we love ourselves implies putting ourselves in the position of the person from whom life support is about to be withdrawn. Ask, with all the honesty you can muster: "What is the most loving thing to do (for the patient, family, community) in this situation?" The same approach is echoed in Augustine's "Love God and do what you will."

Second, in nearly every crisis decision, the Old and New Testaments come down on the side of the needy, dispossessed, and helpless. Determining who is most needy may be difficult. Is it the dying infant, the grieving family, the respirator bound adult, or the anguishing spouse? Along with the love ethic, the presumption in favor of the helpless is indeed a powerful decision-making premise.

This guideline does not imply a bias in favor of maintaining the comatose, incompetent, or dying patient. Indeed, the most loving thing to do may often be to remove the respirator, i.v. or feeding tube and allow the natural healing of death to proceed.

5. Continuity and support. Whether you are the caregiver or the significant other, don't just make the decision and leave. Often families decide to withdraw treatment and then quickly absent themselves from the scene. Likewise caregivers participate as helpers in the high drama of the decision making and then find other things to do.

While the decision is itself important, it is of equal import to back up that decision behaviorally with continuity, contact, and constant support for the patient who is dying as well as for the family or significant other. Be by the bedside of the dying patient or the family who has made a withdrawal or withholding of treatment decision. Agonize with them, cry with them, remember with them as they lie dying. Of course it is difficult to be present as the wishes of the patient or family are carried out, respirators removed, i.v.'s withdrawn, dialysis stopped. But for all involved—patient, family and staff—it is important to support the decision with the dignity with which it was made.

The second major area of critical decision making involves longer term illnesses or disabilities. Situations such as the following require responses slightly different from those listed above.

NON-CRISIS, LONG-TERM SITUATIONS

• Your mother, who has had asthma for thirty years, has been on a respirator for eight weeks. She is alert and conscious, though in end-stage lung disease. She will be discharged to a skilled nursing facility where she will remain until she dies, however long it takes.

• Your 15-week-old fetus has been diagnosed through amniocentesis with a fatal hypoplastic left ventricle. There is a chance you will need a Caesarean section if the fetus develops full term and goes into cardiac distress.

• An employee with whom you work has been diagnosed with AIDS. Even with treatment, he will die within the next several years. You both know that the process is likely to be long and painful.

• Your best friend has just been diagnosed with liver cancer which has metastasized to the brain. She probably has less than six months to live and is refusing any but palliative treatment.

Life support decisions in the context of long-term illnesses have both the luxury and disadvantage of time. While not exerting the pressure that it does in a crisis, time can seem a fearful burden to those faced with the daily chores and demands for decisions it brings.

The recommendations listed for crises (get accurate information, balance needs and wishes, act with disinterest and clarity, act in love/protect the helpless, provide continuity and support) obviously still apply over the long term. The issues are the same, only the time frame in which they are considered has changed. But the longer term nature of the process means that some additional guidelines are necessary.

1. Plan while you can. Whether you are the person who is dying or the helper, consider the options and make the decisions *now*, while still lucid and relatively rational. Even though they have had the time, many patients and their families deny the obvious and avoid making plans or decisions until they are in a crisis.

Business and personal affairs can be put in order, wills and Living Wills filed, treatment decisions made and even funeral arrangements designated before illness (or sudden accident) precludes those choices. (See Chapter 4.) The twofold effect of such discussion and planning is that, once again, the more you have faced these decisions for yourself, the more effective you will be in assisting others to make them.

2. Know the stance of your tradition. If you have a religious tradition that is meaningful to you, find out its stand on the issues of abortion and withholding/withdrawing/refusing life support. Are there any impediments to organ donation or to Living Wills? While you may not necessarily agree with the position of the organization, the information may provide a starting place for discussion and decision making.

3. Loneliness and grief Long-term serious illness is frequently accompanied by an insidious partner—loneliness. As one patient said: "The worst thing about all this is the loneliness." Dying persons usually want and need to talk about their dying, but not in any special or unduly morose manner; yet few people seem to be around who will really listen.

Share the loneliness just as you would share their happiness. Be realistic with patients and families; listen to their stories about the complexities of their lives whether they talk about the bills, the weather, the treatment, the hospital bed, or dying. Listening and spending "normal" time with patients will alleviate the sense of isolation and loneliness that inevitably and repeatedly occurs.

Especially in the long term, be sensitive to and aware of *anticipatory grieving*. Patients may wish themselves dead to unburden their families and avoid pain or a slow death of increasing debilitation. Family members may wish the same and feel guilty about their secret thoughts. Each may begin grieving the loss of the other long before the final stages of death take place.

Be supportive and accepting of the sense of loss, whenever it is felt. Do not discount or reject the feelings by telling the patient or family they "shouldn't feel that way" or by reminding them of "all the time they've had" or have left. You cannot fix or alleviate the feelings of loss, fear, or guilt. You *can* allow persons to express their feelings in your presence without fear of judgment or rejection. And you can express yours with them as well.

4. *Promote educational programs.* As you become more sensitive to the issues faced by dying persons and their caregivers, plan some consciousness-raising activities in your religious organization or through your business or club affiliations. Organize a death planning workshop with speakers from the community on the topics of wills, funeral plans and service options, Living Will legality, and organ donations. Present varying points of view through a series of speakers on ethical issues such as withdrawing/withholding life support, informed consent, artificial organs, and the rationing of health care. The more information people have about an issue or dilemma ahead of time (removing respirators, making funeral plans), the less confused and more clear they will feel about decision making under the pressure of the moment.

Finally, in both crisis and non-crisis decision making there are identical considerations to keep in mind:

1. *Good ethics begin with good facts.* As mentioned earlier, regardless of the time factor, make sure you have the most accurate medical, legal, philosophical, and spiritual information possible. Several opinions are valuable and each perspective will be helpful in making your own personal choice. Listen carefully and caringly to what you are told. Seek clarification and get assistance from friends or other hospital personnel.

2. *What is medically or legally right may not be ethically right.* Just because a procedure is medically "indicated" or legally "propitious" does not mean it is the procedure or action of ethical choice. Decisions have frequently been relegated to the medical and legal communities on the assumption that these groups have some expertise in determining the appropriateness of an action.

Patients and families, especially in a crisis, may turn first to external guidelines from physicians or attorneys hoping to find some solid ground on which to base their opinion of what is "right." Often it is only after some confusing, disappointing or conflicting medico-legal advice that they begin to ask what is "right" for *this* person, given who the person is and what the person wanted.

It seems clear that the basis for moral decision making must be primarily other than legal and medical, though those disciplines may offer helpful information that will affect that decision. The place to start is with the desires of the patient.

3. Can does not imply ought. This clearly revolutionary maxim is nearly un-American. Our country was built on the principle that "can implies ought." If we can built a railroad across the country, we ought to do so. If we can put a person on the moon, in a space station, on another planet, we ought to do it. Our new medical technology, however, is permitting us the ability to do things that in many cases we ought not to do.

Prolongation of life and the prolongation of dying, animal transplants, some reproductive technologies, and other bioethical procedures currently being discussed that will one day be realities will have a profound impact on our societal structure and ways of living and dying. Boundaries will have to be clearly drawn using the above statement as a guide, particularly in the realm of life support decision making.

4. The Bible is not a model for morality; it is a mirror for identity. This favorite saying of Professor William Sanders of Union Theological Seminary indicates that there is not much information about respirators in Genesis or even Leviticus, much less Revelation. Thus it is inappropriate to look to the Bible to tell us specifically what to *do*. It is, however, important for those involved in a religious tradition to view the Bible as a mirror, reflecting commentary and stories to describe who we *are*, what kind of covenant people we are with our peculiar God, and how we interact with God and one another. Using that information will then make our treatment and life support decisions more aligned with the reality of our faith and tradition.

5. All conclusions are provisional. Whatever decision is made has to be considered a provisional one. You may get new test information tomorrow that impacts directly on your choice. (The cancer has not metastasized as was first thought. The infant's abnormality *can* be repaired by a new microsurgical technique.) Likewise, you may get information that opens up (or closes down) a previous avenue of choice. (The surgery is not healing as it should. The chemotherapy is not working. The cobalt is relieving the pain. His appetite is getting better.)

No decision is written in cement. Be open to new information of whatever kind. Convey to patients that you are willing to follow their wishes and keep them informed of progress or the lack of it. Keep updating and asking what their decision is *today*.

The issues we have discussed here are not theoretical or rhetorical ones. The question is not "if" you will have to make these decisions, especially about life support, but "when?" Preparation through education, dialogue, and decision making now will enable you to put those considerations into action when it is your turn to be The Lone Ranger.

III

THE CHURCH AND DEATH

A YEAR'S GRIEF

No red clods now
Ungainly thrown to cover a new grave;
No new grave now —
A year's weathering has worn the soil away,
A year's decay
To coffin and to corpse.

Smooth grass spreads
Where shovel dug to wound and scar the earth.
A standing stone
Tells all that shall be known about this plot
Where rain and rot
Work steadily together.

There can be peace:
Why spurn what makes you fit to fight again?
There can be power:
Give up what was and is, hope and desire,
Kneel at the fire
For this is holy ground.

The mark of death,
Scored on this stone and on our sight, is cross-shaped.
A year ago
The boy we buried here received its grace.
Anoint my face,
Redeem me, Holy One.

K.M.V. Morfey

4

How to Die in the 1990s

Almost daily, those of us who work in healthcare settings see someone die. We assist patients and families with the difficult decisions regarding whether or not to continue treatment in the Emergency Room, whether or not to begin treatment after being diagnosed with a serious or fatal illness, and whether and when to discontinue treatment in adult or neonatal Intensive Care Units and allow death to occur.

In nearly all of these instances patients and families are totally unprepared to make such decisions. They often seek guidance, asking what their options are, trying to decipher the meaning of the complex sounding medical technology and its probability of cure, weighing their feelings about the loved one: their emotions about past attachments or disenchantments, their fear about their own mortality, their hopefulness in continuing their treatment, their guilt at stopping it, their anger and distress at having to decide at all.

Many people act as though death is optional for the human race. But the current crisis in healthcare is bringing home to us the reality of the death of loved ones—young and old—and forcing us to face our own inevitable demise.

The number of persons testing HIV positive is now estimated by the World Health Organization to be one in four hundred. It will reach 25-30 million people by the year 2000, 10 million of whom will be children. AIDS is the leading cause of death of Americans between the ages of 22-44, and the fifth leading cause of death in U.S. women.

The population of aging adults is burgeoning: currently there are over 25,000 Americans over the age of 100; one in eight Americans is over age 65, and by 2020 it will be one in five; the fastest growing age group in this country is that over age 85.

The increasing cost of healthcare (now 12 percent of the GNP) is forcing a total re-evaluation of medical treatment and the way it is provided: over 500 hospitals have closed since 1980; access to care is decreasing, especially in rural areas; insurance and government reimbursements have become severely restricted; many states, such as Oregon, are developing guidelines for healthcare rationing and limits to providing treatment.

These numbers alone mean that each of us will be dealing with the issues of withdrawal of treatment and death in our personal and professional lives with increasing frequency. But the even more important statistic is that eighty percent of deaths occur in health-care institutions. So there is an *eighty percent chance that your death will be decisional—not accidental or natural*. It is extremely difficult to die naturally these days. You can do it, but you have to crawl off somewhere alone and not tell anyone about it—or you have to take the special precautions noted here.

Knowing there is an eighty percent chance that someone else will have to decide how, when, at what cost, where, or in what manner we will die, we can begin now to have discussions and make arrangements that clearly state our preferences when we become incompetent to do so. (Not *if* but *when* we become incompetent.)

MAKING DECISIONS FOR YOURSELF

The following suggestions have grown out of conversations with hundreds of dying patients and their families:

1. *Review your own family history of dealing with death.* Recall the deaths you knew in your family as a child. How were they handled? Did relatives die in the hospital, at home, in a nursing facility? Were you present at those deaths? Were you told about them? How? What do you remember about these occasions?

What were the funerals like in your family? What was said about them? What changes have occurred in the way deaths or funerals have been handled in your family?

Once you have reviewed your family tradition, recall for a moment the deaths of close friends, asking the same questions. Is there anything about those occasions that you would (or would not) like to incorporate into your own planning?

We learn to handle death largely from the traditions passed on to us (verbally or behaviorally) in our own family. But medicine, especially medical technology, has changed the manner of dying since that time, and the assumptions used for decision making by our parents (and even our older siblings) are largely inappropriate for the "high tech death" decisions facing us today in modern healthcare institutions.

The first step toward dying in the 1990s is to examine the assumptions about the meaning and method of death in your family tradition, and then comparing those with your own current beliefs and wishes.

2. Review what you think about death—and life. The focus on death and dying is not really on death at all, but on life. What do you believe about life, your life? What *is* life for you? What *quality of life* is sufficient or right for you?

The "quality of life" question is becoming preeminent as technological options for prolonging body functions increase. Different people will have different criteria for their particular level of desired "quality." For some people a worst-case scenario is being in a wheelchair, incontinent of bowel and bladder, being tube fed and not knowing anyone. For others, being in a persistent vegetative state, or chronically comatose, or having Alzheimer's Disease, or being on artificial interventions (respirator, hydration, nutrition) will overstep the limits of "who they are" (or were) and will mean that treatment should be withdrawn.

The crucial question is: "To *what quality of life* do you want your body resuscitated and/or rehabilitated?" The answer to that question will define who you are, focus on what you believe about life, and make clearer when that "life" is no longer present or desirable. One man, in the Intensive Care Unit for weeks, had a son who was agonizing over what to do and how to decide when to discontinue treatment on his father. Finally, he asked his father for some guideline in this difficult question. His father took his hand and said, "When I'm no longer *me*, stop."

Partly out of concern to do the right thing, and partly as an excuse not to make any decisions, some people ask about those cases when persons who were going to have the artificial interventions shut off actually came out of the coma or experienced sudden recovery or spontaneous remission and went on to live long, healthy lives. As anyone with healthcare experience will tell you, these reports are largely anecdotal, usually apocryphal, and frequently inaccurate. These events do occur, but with nearly minuscule frequency. Although the possibility exists that patients may experience one of these "miraculous cures," it is far more probable that they will not, and decisions need to be based on the best—and most realistic—information available.

Many people will use the "Death myths" explained in Chapter 2 to avoid decisions of withdrawing artificial medical interventions. Others will use their faith as a support in making those same decisions. The important thing in planning is to review and discuss what you believe about God, since your faith will most certainly inform and possibly direct what you want done regarding artificial interventions and funeral planning.

The controversy over the assisted ("suicide machine") death of a 54-year-old Alzheimer's patient in Michigan raises questions about euthanasia, suicide, and assisted suicide. (See Chapter 5.) These issues need to be discussed relative to your view of quality of life and your feelings about hastening death, whether by withdrawal of treatment, or by actively causing death to occur.

3. *Discuss your thoughts and decisions with your family.* Many people have strong feelings and wishes about the use of artificial interventions, either in terms of demanding their use or directing their withdrawal, but such wishes are quite often not honored because of the family's disagreement, direct opposition, or fearful hesitancy to carry out your wishes.

It is very important to discuss your healthcare decisions with your spouse, children, siblings, or significant other. They need to know not only your wishes, but the reasons and feelings supporting those wishes; they need to know that you have heard and taken into consideration their feelings and the feelings of others about you and your life. Most importantly, they need to know that they are supporting and protecting your interests, honoring the person you are, by complying with your requests.

The time to have this conversation (or, more likely, series of conversations) is not at the bedside of an incompetent, comatose ICU patient, but right now while feelings and opinions may be openly, even forcefully stated, so that disagreements may be voiced and decisions made. It may be that consensus will be found in a compromise position, or perhaps the entire family will agree with the wishes of the patient (or future patient). In some cases, owing to total disagreement, you may need to legally designate a separate person to make your healthcare decisions when you become incompetent, to assure that your wishes will be followed. (See Appendix: Durable Power of Attorney for Healthcare.)

4. Discuss your wishes and decisions with your physician. The next person to make aware of your discussions regarding medical treatment during terminal, incurable, or irreversible illness is your family physician. If you don't have one, find one. Call a hospital's physician referral service; nearly all institutions of any size have a computerized listing from which you can choose. It is important to have a primary physician because most extraordinary treatment is done by specialists in a particular field. The internist or family practice physician will act as the gatekeeper and primary admitting doctor for you. Therefore it is vital that this physician know your wishes as explicitly as possible—and agree with them. If the physician does not agree, and if, after exploring the stated objections, you still want your wishes honored, ask that physician for a referral to someone who may be more likely to agree with you, or return to the referral service to change physicians.

As a part of your discussion, state your feelings and opinions regarding the use of artificial hydration (fluids), artificial nutrition (liquid nutrients), and respirators (breathing machines). These are the most likely mechanical devices to be used to maintain body functioning. When is it permissible or desireable to remove artificial hydration and nutrition from you? A breathing machine? Antibiotics? Blood products?

Discuss with your physician the implications and the physiological consequences of removal of each item. Some people react with horror at the idea of patients "dehydrating and starving to death," but neurologists indicate that patients for whom removal of artificial hydration or nutrition is an option either currently have or quickly will have no sensation of hunger or thirst. Thus, maintaining these measures is largely for the comfort of the family or caregiver and often results in prolonging the dying process.

Following the U.S. Supreme Court decision in the Cruzan case in June 1990, each state may determine which artificial interventions it restricts. Missouri, where Nancy Cruzan lay in a persistent vegetative state maintained by hydration and nutrition since 1983, restricts by law the removal of nutrition and hydration. Florida and eight other states do the same. However, the Cruzan decision also determined that nutrition and hydration were "medical treatments" which could be withheld just as any other medical treatment can be, and upheld the right of patients to refuse these and other treatments. Check with your physician or attorney for the laws of your state to be certain your wishes are known, preferably in writing, and will be honored to the full extent of the law.

If your area has a hospice program, you would do well to ask if your physician is affiliated with it or ever uses its services. Such programs are extremely helpful in supporting patients and families through terminal illness, death, and bereavement. They have physician consultants who are knowledgeable in the intricacies of pain management and symptom control, along with volunteers who are trained to be sensitive to psychosocial and spiritual comfort needs. If the patient is on Medicare (and in some states Medicaid), signing into the Hospice program can make a significant difference in percentage of reimbursement provided by the federal government as well as many private insurers.

There is an increasing likelihood that, in coming years, your death will occur at home. As further private and federal payor restrictions are placed on acute care hospitalization, it will probably not be possible to be admitted to a hospital to die. It is, quite simply, too expensive and will not be reimbursed by your insurer or the government. Patients can be palliatively treated at home with services of a home-care nurse at much less expense, and usually with higher quality, dignity, and serenity than in a highly clinical, technologically-oriented acute care institution.

Dying at home requires planning, and will involve state and county laws, especially the directives of the medical examiner (coroner). Because the majority of deaths still take place in healthcare institutions where deaths are part of the daily routine, deaths elsewhere are usually automatically reviewed and perhaps autopsied by the county (or other designated) medical examiner. Often it is a requirement to call Emergency Medical Service (EMS) or the police or fire department to have an official pronouncement of death, after resuscitation measures are attempted, of course.

These requirements have sometimes led to situations ranging from awkward to infuriating, when a family that has just witnessed the death of a loved one at home must now put up with the lights and sirens of police cars, EMS, and fire trucks outside their house, and the sight of emergency medical technicians doing cardiopulmonary resuscitation—and possibly attempting to start i.v.'s and intubation—on the corpse that used to be a family member.

In order to avoid this final insult, the cooperation of your physician is necessary. Discuss this issue and get information about how your county or city system works. Often Hospice is the agency that coordinates the home death with the physician and the local authorities, so that 911 is never called. Usually the patient must have a Living Will, be a hospice patient (sometimes with a hospice nurse present at the death), and be a "known death" so that the physician will agree to sign the death certificate.

Whether dying at home or in a healthcare setting with someone else making treatment decisions, discuss with your doctor your feelings and thoughts about "quality of life." Bring up the difference between doing "everything possible" and "everything necessary" to sustain life, and indicate which one you wish for yourself. (Doing everything necessary does not mean doing everything possible.) Raise the issue of "code status" whenever you are admitted to a hospital for any reason.

Most people do not know that they are issued a "resuscitative code status" upon admission to a healthcare institution. Although exact definitions vary around the country, there are usually three code classifications. Code I is a Full Code: in case of an arrest or cessation of heartbeat or respiration, everything possible will be done to restore and sustain life functions, including CPR (cardiopulmonary resuscitation), medicines, defibrillation (shocking with electronic paddles), and intubation (respirator). Code II means No Heroics: medicines will be used but CPR, intubation, and defibrillation are usually withheld. This code status is appropriate for end stages of diseases or for people who are quite frail and likely to be harmed (broken ribs, punctured lungs) by heroic measures. Code III is a No Code: comfort measures only will be given to maintain pain control, peacefulness, and dignity.

What do you want your Code Status to be upon your next admission to the hospital? On what basis might you want your physician to change your status? Lower it? Raise it?

The more discussion and information your physician has, the more confident you both can be that your wishes will be honored when the appropriate time comes.

5. Create a file of documents. Even though many states honor and uphold the legality of holographic (handwritten) and verbal requests, it is best to have printed and witnessed documents expressing your wishes.

a. Living will Forty-two states have some kind of Natural Death Act. Get a copy from your state Medical Association, or through your physician, hospital chaplain, or social worker. The Society for the Right to Die (250 W. 57th St., New York, NY 10107) can send you a generic one or one specific to your state. As mentioned above, some states restrict withdrawal of treatment to respirators only, arguing that artificial hydration and nutrition are "basic sustenance" and may never be withdrawn. Others, such as Texas, define a "qualified patient" as one with an "incurable or irreversible condition," thus significantly broadening the range of situations covered. Be certain you and your physician know the legal restrictions, so that such treatments may be withheld to begin with and thus need never be withdrawn.

b. Durable Healthcare Power of Attorney Some Living Wills take effect only when the signer is diagnosed with a terminal, or incurable, condition. Thus, if you sign a Living Will when you are healthy, you may have to sign another one *after* you are diagnosed with a fatal condition. But having a Durable Power of Attorney for Healthcare assures that your wishes will be honored whether you are stricken suddenly with a fatal illness, are involved in a critical accident, or develop a terminal condition.

A general Power of Attorney usually becomes invalid *when* you become incompetent. The Durable Power of Attorney for Healthcare does not become valid *until* you become incompetent to make a decision regarding your treatment. In it you designate the person you want to be your decision maker (with usually one or two alternates). This is a very important document to have, and should be witnessed and notarized.

c. Organ donor card Depending on the disease, medical history, cause of death, and age of the patient, a surprising number of organs may be "harvested." Up to age 72, heart valves, skin, corneas, bone, and even some major organs may be available for donation. Multiple organ transplants (heart and lung) and exotic single organ transplants (lung, pancreas) are of such controversy as to lead some commentators to argue that limited healthcare dollars ought not be spent on organ transplants at all. But for the more routine and successful transplants (cornea, kidney, skin, bone marrow), many more donors are needed nationwide to alleviate the suffering experienced by the blind, those on dialysis, and those suffering from burns.

Although some states have clear directives on the back of driver's license cards, the best method of making certain your wishes for donation will be honored is to register with The Living Bank (P.O. Box 6725, Houston TX 77265) or a local organ procurement agency. These organizations maintain computer listings that can be accessed at any hour. Donating your entire body to a medical school can also be arranged through them. Once again, it is important to discuss these decisions with the persons who will be making the ultimate decisions when you are incompetent, since they will have the final say at the time.

d. Funeral plans   Determine what you want done and write it down in detail. Consult with your local clergy if you want a religious service. Pick hymns and readings, and name the persons you want to do things. State your wishes regarding casket, viewing, cremation, scattering of ashes (name the place), and cost of the funeral. Some people will visit a funeral home and make arrangements for themselves. Others argue that it is better to have your arrangements in a file at home so you can update them, and it is better not to pay for a "pre-need" contract when you can put the money in an interest-bearing account designated for your funeral expenses. With such a mobile society, these two considerations are worth heeding.

Along with expressing these preferences in writing, it would be helpful to list account numbers concerning any monetary investments you have, and any other financial or personal information you wish to convey that will affect your funeral directions, if these wishes (e.g., disposition of particular personal items) are not listed in your general will.

Finally, make certain that a copy of this file, with all the documents dated, is given to your next of kin (significant other, or person designated to make your healthcare decisions). Your physician, attorney, clergy, and anyone else you think appropriate should, of course, have copies of your Living Will, Durable Power of Attorney for Healthcare, and Organ Donor Card.

6. Annual review of decisions   Mark a significant date on your personal calendar—birthday, anniversary, holiday—and on that date, annually review all of your decisions. Update information where appropriate, redate documents, and send them to the persons who received the original files. New information, new circumstances, or further thought may move you to change your mind. In any case, take the time to update regularly.

MAKING DECISIONS FOR OTHERS

Death is no respecter of age or convenience. Still, many younger people believe that they will not have to face death and related issues in the 1990s. They are wrong. They will have to make decisions for parents, aging relatives, siblings, and perhaps for themselves and their children.

Traditionally the two ways of making such decisions have been through determination of "best interests" and "substituted judgment." The first asks: What is in Dad's best interests? Is it better to continue treatment or to cease? Is it in Mother's best interests to die? The second method asks the decision makers to put themselves in the patient's position and make a decision as if they were the patient. It asks: What would this person decide if she or he could sit up in the bed and tell us what to do?

Both questions have merit. They are made substantially easier when the patient has done the work mentioned above. But if no records are present and no discussion has passed between patient, physician, and family, one might need to go beyond the concepts of "best interests" and "substituted judgment."

A third and newly developed method is that of "inclusive interests." Developed by Russell Hoverman, M.D. and the author, this method argues that, especially in cases where no previous conversation or documentation has occurred, one cannot really know what is now in the best interest of the patient and cannot put oneself in the position of the patient to make a decision on something never discussed. Rather, what the decision maker can do is to consider the interests of all parties involved: patient, family, physician, staff, and community.

• Patient: What was the life of this person like? Who was she? What kind of decisions did she make in other critical situations or other areas of business and personal life? What decision regarding continuation or termination of treatment would be consistent with those decisions and that style of living?

• Family: What are their feelings about this person? What will be the result for them if or when the death occurs? How will they feel about making that decision? Do they need or want more time? More information? More discussion?

• Physician/Staff/Community: The healthcare team has an interest in "doing no harm," in allocating healthcare resources conservatively, appropriately using technology to avoid forcing an unfair financial burden on anyone, either the patient or family or the institution (which will have to cover losses not met by insurance or family).

"Inclusive interests" decision making considers the situations of everyone involved, seeks to equitably weigh the benefits and burdens to each party, and come to a decision that is in the best interests of all.

If there is any dispute between the parties, or another objective opinion is desired, it is appropriate for the hospital Ethics Committee to be consulted. Nearly every hospital has its own Ethics Committee, consisting of persons from the community, the institution, and from different professions and interests, with expertise in healthcare, law, ethics, religion, social services, psychology, and other relevant areas. Usually sought through Pastoral Care or Social Services, the Ethics Committee reviews the patient's case, talks with physicians, family, caregivers, and (often with the family present) discusses and comes to some consensus about what course of action to take.

The consensus of the committee is never binding. It is yet another resource for determining "inclusive interests" and offers a considered opinion the family and physician can then add to their deliberations. These people may then follow the course suggested by the committee, reject it, or develop some variation of it. In nearly every case, however, the recommendation of the committee is able to satisfy the needs and interests of all parties, since the function of the group is not to be adversarial but consultative.

For severely disabled patients, the mentally retarded, and those with no family or guardians, review by the facility Ethics Committee is usually mandatory.

As the 1990s progress, the trends toward restricted allocation of healthcare resources will only increase. Ironically, so will the medical technology that is largely responsible for the need for those restrictions.

So as not to be trapped between the rock of allocation and the hard place of technology, it is in our own best interests and the best interests of our family, significant others, and healthcare givers, to have discussions *now* about our wishes, our preferences, and our demands regarding limits to our care.

If we do not, we relegate those decisions, and the entire decision making process, to public policy makers over whom we have little bureaucratic control and who are likely to have other biases and concerns than ours.

Now is the only time we have to discuss these issues; now is the only time we have to make our desires known, our wishes clear; now is the only time we have to plan for our dying, so that we might live, and live fully, from now until then.

5

Hastening
the Inevitable

When is it all right to kill yourself?
When is it permissible to cause or allow another's death? Under
what conditions or circumstances is it ethical to assist someone to
accomplish his or her own death? Up until very recently these
questions were answered quickly and with relative ease: Never.
Never. None. It was only in the extreme instance that possible scenarios could be conceived where such actions might be reluctantly
acceptable: to save the life of another during wartime conditions, to
hasten one's death under circumstances of torture, severe war injury, or unbearable accident-induced pain.

But medical technology has created situations in hospitals, intensive care units, and nursing homes across the country in which patients in various stages of debilitation, unconsciousness, indignity,
and suffering are cared for while under siege from the incredible in-
struments of mechanized life we have devised. Our technology
now supplants vital functions, extending what is ostensibly "life"
beyond the normal limits of compromised organs.

In some instances, where there is a need for such temporary sub-
stitution of organs or organ functions, the technology is *life-saving:*
it allows the body to continue functioning while a machine breathes
for lungs, pumps for a heart, provides nutrients or hydration when
ingestion, swallowing, or digestion is impossible. But for persons in
an incurable or irreversible condition, the technology is often *death-
prolonging*. It is clear from the repeated comments of patients, par-

ticularly of older persons, that what is feared most is not death itself, but the possibility of prolonged attachment to medical devices that merely sustain bodily functioning.

The ultimate question now is not *"Will* I die?" but *"How* will I die?" Even, "In what state of *indignity* will I die?" In the balancing of burdens and benefits, the loss of dignity is often of more concern than the inevitable death.

To exercise some control over a healthcare system that seems bent on sustaining life at all costs and to avoid spending one's last days and hours as an impersonal attachment at the end of a machine, many people are exploring the concept of euthanasia. Literally meaning "good death," euthanasia is characterized by its proponents as a means of aggressively maintaining control of one's life and death, rather than passively accepting the seemingly limitless presumptions of medicine. Euthanasia is thought to be a way to maintain some remnant of dignity in the face of the usual and unusual indignities of "high-tech" death practiced in the United States. It is a way of actively setting limits on treatment so as to die in a "timely" fashion, in contrast to "natural" death which requires allowing the disease or disability to ravage the body, or mechanical death (allowing ravaging while attached to machines), both of which seem to some interminable (no pun intended). Finally, euthanasia is thought to value quality of life rather than the quantity of hours or days for the sake of life and life alone.

Opponents of euthanasia consider it a sign of hopelessness that any natural or miraculous recovery is possible; persons who desire it are judged to have thoughtlessly "given up" too soon. It is, in this view, a selfish endeavor, demanding death on one's own terms, wasting the potential for moments of happiness for the ill person or family, and sacrilegiously usurping God's prerogative to determine how and when one dies.

There is further disagreement on whether there is any difference between "active" and "passive" euthanasia. Some argue that removing a respirator is an "action" and therefore constitutes actively causing the death of the patient. Others say that removing the respirator and "allowing" death to occur simply gets the technology out of the way and permits the natural process of death to proceed.

This "getting out of the way" is considered "passive" euthanasia.

There is also a middle ground, the standard practice of permitting "tangential euthanasia." Narcotic and other pain relievers are knowingly and ethically administered to terminal patients for whom the result will be to further reduce their respirations and hasten death. The intent is not death but pain control, and it is unconscionable *not* to offer relief from that pain for fear of hastening death.

It is clear that there is a difference between active and passive euthanasia. To argue otherwise is to play word games. Passively removing interventions and allowing death to occur has a different moral, intuitive feel than purposely causing that death, e.g., with a gun or a lethal injection. Tangential euthanasia is still passive, since its aim is to relieve pain, not cause death. The goal in managing the terminal patient is to alleviate suffering; for these patients there is less suffering in death than in being forced to endure further pain. Likewise the traditional medical goal to "do no harm" is upheld by pain and symptom control rather than by aggressively imposing further discomforts.

The difficulty in defining what we mean by "active," "passive," "tangential," and even "euthanasia" itself, indicates an important historical occurrence. *Our medical technology has outpaced not only our ethical system but our vocabulary to describe what we do.* We can now keep bodies functioning for longer and longer periods of time, beyond the point where they would have died or been considered dead twenty years ago. Our old descriptions of what one's condition is as well as what to do about it no longer accurately depict the situation. For instance:

• "Euthanasia" was traditionally considered to be a reluctant "mercy killing" of a dying or disabled person, not unlike shooting a horse or putting down an animal to avoid unnecessary misery or suffering. The new definition includes the concept of a merciful death, but goes beyond the rationale of misery and suffering to include relief from unwarranted medical prolongation of incurable and irreversible conditions. In fact, euthanasia has taken on new meaning because the word "suffering" itself has done so.

• "Suicide" used to describe the immoral and unwarranted taking

ing of one's own life, usually with a sense of hostility, defiance, or despair. Today it may mean anything from the ethical refusal of treatment to the planned self-inflicted death of a person with an incurable or irreversible condition, often with a sense of triumph, dignity, and control.

• "Murder," until recently, was thought in the medical arena to be the causing of, or purposely allowing, the death of another. Now these actions are called "withdrawal of artificial interventions," "pain management," and possibly even "assisted suicide."

"Death" used to be defined as "cessation of heartbeat and respiration." Now, "whole brain death" may describe a body in which a heart beats and lungs exchange oxygen and carbon dioxide. "Neocortical brain death" (cessation of function of the higher cortical areas of the brain) describes the "death of the 'person,'" as in a persistent vegetative state, or end-stage Alzheimer's Disease.

Clearly, new words are needed and will develop as the old ones either take on entirely new meaning, or evolve into more descriptive terms. In the meantime, it may be helpful for purposes of discussion to combine the terms euthanasia, murder, suicide, and assisted suicide under the phrase "hastening the inevitable."

The word "hastening" is carefully chosen. It is ironically akin to "quickening." If quickening is an indication of a desired life, hastening is an indication of a desired death. The word also has a softness to it that conveys a sense of welcome, of caring, of consideration for the life and values of the afflicted person. It serves to contrast the harsh, sterile, prolonged high-tech death that many face as the alternative.

Other words will arise through further discussion and debate. One leader in this field, J. Russell Hoverman, M.D., suggests we need verbs, not nouns ("hastening," not "euthanasia") to describe that what we are doing involves process, not conclusion. The theological parallels are obvious here. We are in constant process with our God, interacting as we grow and learn together, even developing new language by which to know and relate to each other. We are never in rigid conclusion about God (whose Hebrew name is a verb), and we ought never to be in rigid conclusion on the ethical issues that we discuss here.

PASSIVE HASTENING

Getting out of the way and allowing death to occur may take many forms. One may choose to refuse treatment from the very onset of symptoms or initial diagnosis of a terminal condition. It is also possible to refuse or withdraw treatment at any point along the way from diagnosis to death. Contrary to the belief of many healthcare practitioners, it is plainly ridiculous to assume that "once a treatment is started, it cannot be stopped" or is more difficult to stop. If *any* treatment is begun and found to be useless or harmful (without overriding benefit), it is to be stopped, whether the treatment is antibiotics, blood products, medications, or mechanical devices. In fact, one could argue that under such circumstances there is a moral obligation to stop.

This does not mean, however, that care is withdrawn. Stopping aggressive treatment means changing the goal of treatment from curative to palliative, from restoring health to enhancing the dignity, pride, comfort, and ease of the patient and family. The controversy arises in determining *when* such passive hastening is begun.

Most people have little difficulty withdrawing respirators, artificial hydration, and nutrition when death is imminent. For others, the inevitability of outcome, combined with the ultimate futility of treatment, emotional and financial costs, expected side effects of therapies, and, most importantly, quality of life interests (communication, mobility, control of bodily functions, thought, lucidity) lead them to opt for palliative care as early as the initial diagnosis.

The courts have generally recognized the legal right of persons to refuse treatment and to request "passive hastening," especially if there is a written directive to that end (Living Will or Durable Power of Attorney for Healthcare). The medical community is also starting to recognize the same prerogative for the patient and sees it in accord with the physician's duty to "relieve suffering," "to do no harm," and to cease prolonging the dying process. It remains for the church to fully endorse the ethical nature of such decisions—at any point on the spectrum of irreversible or incurable conditions.

ACTIVE HASTENING

Due to the advancement of biomedical technology, there are currently and will continue to be situations where the active hastening of death is appropriate.

• A woman learns through an ultrasound at 34 weeks that her baby has anencephaly (no upper brain), a condition incompatible with life. She wishes to induce delivery now rather than be forced to carry the fetus to term.

• An AIDS patient knows that his otherwise strong body and organs will take a month to slowly, painfully deteriorate, gradually reducing him to total dependency as he becomes more skeletal, dehydrates, has seizures, becomes demented, and dies. He wishes to die now, while his dignity and faculties are still intact.

• An advanced Alzheimer's patient develops pneumonia, refuses food, knows no one. His wife of 53 years refuses to allow insertion of a gastrostomy (feeding) tube. She wishes to hasten her husband's death now, as he had requested when he was first diagnosed, and had consistently stated until he was incapable of understanding anyone.

• A head injury or stroke patient faces the prospect of long-term rehabilitation, the end result of which will be the ability to sit in a wheelchair, incontinent of bowel and bladder, artificially fed and hydrated, with minimal interaction with her family. They believe it is consistent with her (undocumented) wishes and lifestyle to cause her immediate death now, rather than force her to "live" in this condition.

These four illustrations are paradigmatic of current dilemmas created by our otherwise immensely helpful medical technology. We have ventured into territory unknown before and find ourselves in situations that our words do not accurately describe, where otherwise obvious ethical and moral guidelines (such as "Do not kill") no longer prevail, and where we must make decisions that seem intuitively right, even though they are extremely dangerous if not carefully circumscribed and severely limited.

It must be possible to develop guidelines, which are ethically, medically, and legally sound, to enable patients to circumvent the current system of medically obligatory high tech–low dignity, high expense–low quality prolonged living/dying. It must be possible to replace that model with the *option* of high-dignity, high-quality, comfortable, life-affirming, active hastening of death. In the Netherlands, for example, there are five criteria for such active hastening. Patients must:

- be terminally ill (certified by two physicians)
- make the request themselves
- be in intractable pain
- make the request over time
- be found to be in good mental health.

If such criteria are met, they may apply to their physician and receive a lethal injection. It is estimated that between ten and twenty thousand deaths a year are hastened there in this manner.

Because the United States is a more heterogenous culture (and the most litigious in the world), we might start with the Dutch criteria and require additional guidelines such as the following:

- A written directive clearly stating the desires of the patient must be in evidence. It would perhaps be best if the directive had been in effect for some period of time preceding the need for it, but current wishes recently written and clearly stated should, in any case, be honored. In most situations a Living Will and Durable Power of Attorney for Healthcare would suffice. But perhaps there is a need for the development of a Durable Power of Attorney for Hastening, indicating the name of the agent who would make that decision if the patient were unable to do so. Further, there may be a need for legal designation of the person to assist in the hastening (excluding relatives, direct healthcare providers, and those who stand to inherit.)

- Anyone assisting in the hastening process at the written request of the dying patient must be immune from criminal prosecution. Such assistance must be carefully spelled out and limited to physical intervention when the patient is no longer physically or mentally capable of carrying out his or her own wishes.

- Likewise, anyone assisting in the hastening process must be immune from civil lawsuit, as must be the patient. (Further limitations on the one who assists must be developed: e.g., assistants must not be related or stand to inherit.)

- Insurance companies must be directed by law to honor the existing life insurance policies of patients hastening their own deaths.

Such companies must not be permitted to consider these actions "suicide," therefore negating the payment of the policy.

- Unless the condition is the result of sudden accident or acute illness, there must be evidence that the patient's estate is in good order, to indicate that the decision is not precipitous and takes into account the persons who will be left behind.

- There may be letter(s) of evidence from friends or family to the effect that this decision is consistent with the life of the patient. The absence of such information should not preclude the personal choice of active hastening, but if possible, such evidence would substantially add to the credibility of the decision.

- There may be need to further develop the concept of an ethics committee, using the current hospital ethics committee model of interdisciplinary representation, to discuss each individual application for active hastening in a relatively public forum, just as hospital ethics committees now are asked to review decisions to withhold or withdraw life-sustaining interventions. Active hastening in healthcare institutions could be handled through existing ethics committees. Requests for active hastening at home could be reviewed by an ethics committee established through the home healthcare agency, an affiliated hospital or nursing facility, the physician's practice group or large clinic, or perhaps even a community ethics committee, functioning just as city-wide institutional review boards (for the protection of human subjects in research protocols) do now. Such ethics committees must be constructed and procedurally designed to preclude bureaucracy, which often results from good intentions. Perhaps they are unnecessary if the laws are clear. What is needed is a process that preserves the individual's freedom and right to privacy (including the right to be left alone), yet allows the state to legally protect meaningful life.

With these guidelines in place, along with other safeguards that would need to be developed, federal/state guidelines may then be designed to specifiy when the hastening of death is *prohibited*, when it is *permissible*, and when it is *obligatory*. It is relatively easy to conceive of situations—not life-threatening or life-recovering—where active or passive hastening would be prohibited. We have already discussed a number of instances where both might be permissible. The last category, obligatory, seems more appropriately confined to passive hastening (in cases of brain death or other evidence of futility of curative treatment). It is reasonable to surmise that there are situations where aggressive treatment would be proscribed and the passive hastening of death would be obligatory. Physicians already seem to welcome the concept of being prohibited from offering extensive, expensive, extraordinary treatments in situations that they and other medical professionals know will be futile.

Also, there are some disease or accident conditions and neonatal anomalies that by definition (incompatible with life, always terminal, grossly self-destructive, 100 percent death rate) would rightly fall under the category of obligatory active hastening. Even so, the dangers of such a requirement currently seem to far outweigh the presumed benefits. Such an (active) option must always be permissible but never required if we are to maintain the protection of liberty that our society has traditionally honored and upheld.

The church's historic condemnatory stance on these issues is based on data that knows little of the extremes created by current and future biomedical technology. The traditional sanctity of life arguments no longer apply when we are faced with new situations that look like "life" but are not, such as persistent vegetative states, comas, brain-dead bodies with minimal brain stem function, and numerous congenital or drug-induced anomalies. We must come to terms with the fact that some of the "life" we have created or into which we have ventured is *not* sacred, that is, in need of protection and preservation at all costs.

In fact, the opposite is true. To truly preserve what it has traditionally held to be the "sanctity of life," the church must become a willing partner in the development of carefully circumscribed guidelines to permit the passive and active hastening of death. To do less than that is to capitulate responsibility to medical technology and to condemn people to horrid deaths to which we would not submit our animals.

H. Tristram Engelhardt, Ph.D., M.D. of the Center for Ethics, Medicine and Public Issues, has written of the papal guidelines of the year 1595 under which medical treatment could be refused.

These included balancing the usefulness of treatment against social and economic cost, amount of pain, inconvenience, and *"horror magnus."* If the cost was more than the average person made in an average year, if the pain of treatment was greater than one wanted to endure, if the treatment meant uprooting or leaving one's family and losing employment, or if the remedy caused considerable revulsion, then the person need not submit to treatment. Four hundred years later, these guidelines may still apply, not only to medical treatment but to determining the required continuance or allowable ending of life.

The stance of the church, then, must be one of guidance, counsel, support, permission, absolution, mercy, acceptance, and forgiveness; in short, it must hold to traditional sacramental stance. It must indeed *be there* before, after, and especially during the time of the hastening to provide sacramental and personal presence consistent with the presence provided at the other transitions of the person's life.

To accomplish all this concerning hastening the inevitable will require much study and debate, the formation of new vocabulary, and the careful fashioning of guidelines that are mercifully fair and socially just. Even more important, it will require the courage to follow the Holy Spirit in the development of a new moral understanding of who we are as the church in the world today, if that church is to have any meaning at all.

6

Death Planning— Church Denial

She stands by the bed watching her husband breathe and listening to the gurgling in his lungs. Hanging onto life is such work. She holds his hand and gently strokes what remains of his once beautiful, thick white hair. The chemotherapy has reduced it to strands; but she lovingly pats him, kisses him, tells him she loves him as she has always done.

The interval between gasps for breath lengthens. Ten seconds, 15 seconds, 30 seconds—forever. She calls for the nurse who searches for and cannot find a heartbeat. The nurse leaves to summon a doctor to make the medical pronouncement. The dead man's wife breaks down and sobs.

Then the questions begin.

What plans have you made for the body? Do you have a funeral home in mind? Do you want cremation? What kind of service do you prefer? How much do you want to pay for the funeral service? What about embalming? Have you talked with your clergy about the plans? Will you sign this form to release the body, please?

And the answers are usually the same.

"I don't know. We never talked about it. Does our church

allow cremation? I wonder what his wishes were. My church never taught me about funerals. Do I need to call my clergy? What do I do next?"

The scenario portrayed here is familiar to anyone working with dying patients and their families. People come into the hospital either in the final stages of disease or in the midst of a medical crisis and die quickly or unexpectedly. Family members are then at a total loss as to what ought to be done. Their religious affiliation has not prepared them for this moment.

Often, conflicting wishes or beliefs lead to serious arguments at a time when closeness, consolation, and mutual support are needed. Sometimes decisions are made in the rush of the moment that are later regretted. Such issues as embalming, the use of make up, closed or open casket, and cremation are very emotionally laden. If not handled carefully, they can provide the basis for years of resentment and separation.

Frequently, no one has ever talked to the deceased about specific wishes concerning funeral arrangements even though the person has been sick for some time. The conspiracy of silence regarding the family member's illness and dying then results in the availability of far fewer options which are now chosen under less than rational circumstances.

There are, of course, many cultural biases in favor of denying the inevitability of death and the obvious need for plans to be made (regardless of age or situation) to prepare for that certainty. There is, however, another source of reluctance to deal with death planning. The church (meaning here the entire religious community in this country, regardless of denomination or sect) has consistently been a willing partner in this cultural avoidance in two ways.

1. Non-affiliation   The clear majority of patients, families and staff in the hospital have no church or clergy affiliation. A recent Gallup poll revealed that only about 40 percent of Americans claimed any such relationship with church or clergy, although most people state a religious *preference* on their hospital admission data sheet. Often the hospital's Pastoral Care personnel are the first contact with religion the patient or family has had in years.

Most people do report religious training of some kind, usually with anecdotal stories of church meetings, Bible school teachers, and religious authority figures, most of which come across as alternately stern, overwhelming, or ludicrous. It is clear that religious education, as the child's first impression of what spirituality is about, leaves much to be desired.

Even if the early exposure was meaningful, the current experiences they have had in churches (particularly regarding illness and death) have been unfavorable or, worse, irrelevant. From the feelings expressed by hospitalized patients, it seems that the real spiritual needs of individuals and families are frequently not being met in the parish church.

For those who are involved in local churches, this serious indictment of the meaning and efficacy of parish programs may come as a surprise and even may be greeted with some anger. But it is hard to discount the feelings of patients who, at a time when they desperately need some internal and external spiritual resources, find that they have none. For this lack of support, education, and spiritual training, the church must bear some culpability.

2. Church-supported denial It would be easy to assume that unaffiliated persons having no church contact would be less knowledgeable about rituals, procedures, and appropriate behavior before, during and after the death. It is interesting, however, that even those persons who are weekly attenders, devout Christians and Jews, and whose clergy come to visit regularly in the hospital are often equally frustrated, uninformed, and unprepared for the onslaught of questions to be answered and decisions to be made.

Clearly the church has, both overtly and covertly, participated in and reinforced its parishioners' denial of death. Furthermore, by failing to deal effectively with the issues of death planning and dying, through education, preaching, worship and witness, the church has downplayed and discounted its own very powerful message about how to *live*. This denial by the church has taken three forms: *Practical, Theological, and Sacramental.*

1. Practical denial Few persons have been taught by their local parish the practical details of what to do when they or someone they love is about to die. As a result, people seldom know their particular church's rituals or liturgies surrounding dying, including what prayers might be appropriate at the time of death. Whether and how to call for clergy, which funeral home to use, whether or not to embalm or to consider cremation, and whether to have the service (if there is to be one) in the church or funeral home are practical matters that have largely been ignored by the church.

Organ and body donations, extraordinary means of life support, and decisions about withholding, withdrawing, or refusing medical treatment are issues that could be addressed by informed clergy and laity _before_ the need for definitive action arises.

Although local physicians, memorial societies, and funeral directors would welcome the chance to provide such information along with clergy, they are seldom asked to do so by the church. Thus the practical matters surrounding death remain a mystery to most parishioners until such time as they are forced to discover them.

2. _Theological denial_ This kind of denial by the church is perhaps more regrettable than the reluctance to deal with practicalities of dying. It is primarily due to poor or nonexistent theological teaching that most people (churched and unchurched) believe that "good is always rewarded and evil always punished." If that is true, it is easy to see how people might conclude that those who are prosperous and healthy must therefore be living good lives, while those who are sick or deteriorating must have done something wrong.

Hospital staff are frequently asked the question "If good is rewarded and evil punished, why is my good, kind, Christian husband lying here dying in excruciating pain?" Of the many usual responses to that question, none is satisfactory. There are some theological approaches to the problem that are helpful in dealing with what appears to be illogical tragedy. Unfortunately, because illness and death are seldom wrestled with in the pulpit or church classroom, parishioners are left to face these crises with the usual meaningless cultural platitudes that leave them feeling empty and unresolved.

Mixing together the issues of good/evil with sickness/punishment, many people assume that their sickness is a punishment for something they have done or not done. An unfortunate result of this largely unexamined theological assumption is a cycle of anger and guilt. They feel frustrated and angry at God because of the pain, shock, or unfairness of their illness but are prevented from expressing those feelings due to poor theologizing by the church ("It's not permitted to be angry at God.") These persons then end up feeling guilty about feeling angry about feeling punished.

The daughter of a dying patient experienced just this emotional cycle. After much discussion she was relieved to have her angry feelings affirmed without risking alienation or punishment. It was helpful to her to acknowledge that she could feel angry and frustrated at God while still trusting God.

There is indeed a wealth of theological literature available on the subjects of illness and death. The church, however, has almost universally ignored it, to the detriment of patients and their families who are or will be in times of crisis.

3. Sacramental denial The church's refusal to teach its people to deal with death sacramentally is a direct result of the expropriation of power and authority from religion to medicine. In the overwhelming popular presence of "miracle drugs," microsurgery, and biomedical technology, the church has increasingly discounted the efficaciousness of its own sacraments.

Holy Communion, anointing, and laying on of hands, intercessory prayer, confession, absolution, and baptism into the covenant community are, or could be, powerful resources for patients and families to confront the reality of dying. The church's witness to the presence of God in whatever form healing may take, including death, could be a valuable tool in the treatment of illness and in sustaining and nourishing those who are dying.

Unfortunately, the religious community does not take its sacraments seriously enough to offer them with the confidence and assertiveness that the medical community offers theirs. Confession and communion are not believed to be as powerful as cobalt and chemotherapy. Anointing and absolution are seen as less effective than medication and surgery.

By taking an extremely narrow view of "healing," limiting it to visible, physiological change, the church has allowed the mystique of medicine to supplant its own holy mysteries and to become the treatment of choice, often to the exclusion of religious ministrations to the ill and dying.

The medical community, on the other hand, usually treats religious and sacramental resources with more respect than the church itself. Physicians, nurses, and other healthcare personnel regularly refer patients and families to Pastoral Care staff and parish clergy to offer the kind of healing resources which medicine cannot provide. It is as though the medical community, far from being competitive or critical, is calling on the church to *be* the church, to exercise its proper, historical function and to do what mere medicine cannot—to support, sustain, transcend, and offer healing to the *whole* person in body, mind, and spirit.

The reasons leading up to the church's threefold denial in death planning are also threefold:

• Clergy and lay conspiracy
• Resurrection theology
• Cultural capitulation

1. Clergy and lay conspiracy Clergy are no different from anyone else when it comes to death. They have the same fears, hopes, apprehensions, and fantasies as the lay persons with whom they minister. Often, therefore, an unwritten agreement develops between the two not to talk about illness and death until the need arises.

As has been stated earlier, in order to offer programs, seminars, workshops, or sermons about death and dying, clergy (like others) must be somewhat comfortable with their own finitude. To talk about the death of others raises the issue of our own. To get into the specifics of funeral planning for others raises the spectre of our own demise.

Frequently clergy are reluctant to offer practical, theological, and sacramental perspectives on death and dying due to their own discomfort about dealing with their own mortality. Supported and reinforced in this behavior by an equally fearful laity, the conspiracy leads to the problems noted above in time of medical crisis.

2. Resurrection theology To focus on resurrection theology is to talk of new life here and now, and of an afterlife where "we will all meet up yonder." It can be uplifting, hopeful, positive and encouraging. It can also be a way to discount and deny the sadness, brokenness, and finality of the end we all must face.

This theological orientation has its basis in the usual Good Friday sermons. On a day appropriate for mourning, anger, sadness, and grief, clergy and laity alike quickly skip over, ignore, or treat shallowly the painful, agonizing transition of Christ Jesus' death on Good Friday in their hurry to get to the positive feelings associated with Easter.

Practically, this resurrection theology takes the form of denying death, demanding cheerfulness and strength in the face of helpless deterioration, and covering sadness with a veneer of forced happiness. The unreality of this approach is so painfully clear to most people going through bereavement that they reject out of hand the source (the church and its teachings) from which it comes.

Congregations which follow this belief system are unlikely to deal with the issues of illness and death in ways that encourage the expression of pain, doubt, depression, or sadness. Until such groups deal with their own fear of death, they are also unlikely to understand the fullest meaning of the Crucifixion and the balance and depth it brings to the experience of Resurrection.

3. *Cultural capitulation*   Due to the church's own discounting of the value and efficacy of its sacraments and theology, a gradual change in allegiance has occurred. Instead of following the tenets of the church, which now have fallen into disfashion, both clergy and laity have begun following popular social methods of dealing with illness, dying, and death. The church has quietly acquiesced to cultural norms, such as preferring that death occur in sterile hospitals and that final religious services be held in equally sterile funeral homes. The docile acceptance of these practices has meant a capitulation of responsibility for death planning to cultural caretakers and a virtual exclusion of church presence at two important times of impact, the death and the funeral. Physicians and healthcare workers manage the death. Funeral directors orchestrate the burial.

Two recent trends may wrest these events away from the grip of the cultural caretakers, and provide the opportunity for the church to regain its position of priority and responsibility in affecting the place and the rituals of death. The recent growing interest in Hospice care for the terminally ill could refocus death in a more personal setting, with opportunity for church and family ministrations. And the new concern for "simple burial" and/or cremation may result in greater involvement on the part of clergy and others inde-termining appropriate rituals (and the sacramental place of those rituals) surrounding such desires.

The importance of death planning, especially for the community of the church, is clear. It is a logical outgrowth of the church's relig-ious commitment and belief. It is the natural result of a fair balance of both resurrection and crucifixion theology. It is the necessary topic of practical, theological, and sacramental involvement in the life and death of the community.

Both clergy and laity alike have a number of options available to enable them to explore the meaning of their own death and the manner in which they would prefer to plan for it. Some of those op-tions are: *Read, Discuss, Decide, Encourage,* and *Live.*

Read Read about illness, death, and dying. Read about how oth-ers have grappled and coped with it. Experience with those writers the confusion, the whole range of feelings from anger to resignation to protest to fear, and the resolution, if any, they or their loved ones found in that process.

Read about the various options for death planning, including bu-rial, cremation, simple funeral, and the scattering of ashes. Read about the ethics of dying, of euthanasia, of suicide, of discontinu-ing, withholding, or refusing all but palliative care. Read about Hospice and how it helps those who are dying to live every day of their lives as much as they are able. Read whatever interests you on the subject and as you read...

Discuss Discuss with friends and family what you've read. Share the feelings raised in you as you read and contemplate your own death. Talk with your physician about how medical decisions are made and with your clergy about the church's position on abortion, life support, dying at home, and funeral practices such as embalm-ing, cremation, scattering of ashes and burial. Discuss the meaning of your own denomination's funeral service, the sacraments and their meaning in life and death, the theology of guilt, forgiveness, sickness, punishment, healing, and death. Perhaps most important-ly, discuss with your loved ones their and your wishes concerning your death and as you talk....

Decide Decide on your own funeral plans. Make determinations about a Living Will, a healthcare power of attorney, a last will and testament, and body organ donations. Pick out the hymns, readings, and other service items you want included at your funeral. Make a visit with your family or clergy to a funeral home to discuss what options you might want. Some people make prearrangements with a particular funeral home; others, given the mobility of our society, set aside money in a separate account to accumulate interest, designated for use on their funeral.

As you make these decisions, write down your wishes and go over them with your family members so they will know what to do when the time comes. After you decide, or as you are deciding...

Encourage Encourage others in the church to do likewise. You will find that many people share your concern and have been equally reluctant to discuss their own death with anyone. You may find they are relieved to have someone to talk to who is willing to listen and take them seriously. Encourage the formation of a study group whose goal would be to have members plan their own funerals.

Encourage and take the lead in setting up a conference or workshop on options for dying to raise the consciousness of other parishioners. Encourage and support your clergy to preach, teach, and witness to the practical, theological, and sacramental aspects of illness and death.

Finally, in the midst of all the experiences of death:

Live Live one day at a time. Live hopefully, rather than optimistically. The Judeo-Christian tradition is not *optimistic* about life and death; it is *hopeful*—hopeful that death is an end but not *the* end, a last word but not *the* last word, the end of one life and beginning of another. Optimism denies death and discounts disease; hope affirms death and transcends disease.

In the Episcopal tradition there is a prayer for the funeral liturgy that sums up the meaning of integrating the issues of illness and death into our everyday experience. The prayer encourages us to "live as those expecting to die and to die as those expecting to live." Such an attitude, contrary to the current popular practice of the church, will result in a realistic appraisal and action orientation regarding the issue of death planning.

JUNE 18, 1983

Who killed you,
You who lie dying by the twisted metal
Stretched on the pavement that smashed your skull
Twitching in your senseless agony?
Surrounded by your courtiers—that passing crowd
Who knew you, saw your danger
(But not how it was caused, if that would comfort me),
Ran at the insane screech of brakes and tires,
Beheld you graceful in the air before so great a fall,
And now wait murmuring—
Prince of your life
I must deny a crown for you in mine.

Who killed you, you or the man in the car
Who stayed awhile but fled from questioning?
Would that I had, that I might blame myself and know
    searing forgiveness;
Yet I must plead not guilty to killing you—
Guilty only of smothering and crowning you in retro-
    spect
By asking insistently to know
By requiring of God to answer me
Who killed you.

You must be free from me and from my question.
You needed me to stroke your hand and speak to you
When you were dying;
You needed me to pray with you and stay with you
So you might find the good and easy way
To that far country;
But not this question, it was not needed then.
I never thought to ask until
Grieving how you were gone from me
And goaded by others' curiosity and by their needs

I started to immure you in my life
And make a puppet-ruler of you there
(An ancient tendency, against which you and I had often
    fought together)
By requiring obsessively an answer to this unanswerable
    question.

I must give all; it is required of me not to know.
(You tell me so and fight in me again the possessive
    craving.)
It lies between you and Him Who judges all
Into whose mercy you have already moved;
The case is shut and I am turned away.
How else could you be free to be
Undefeated as the young David was
Triumphant over Goliath's head
Glorious in victory?

K.M.V. Morfey

7

Theology
By Slogan

Emma Hawley lies dying in room 423. Her family stands around her bed, watching and waiting. She is no longer responsive, but they all keep talking to her, holding her hand, loving her.

Symbols of her life surround them; her Bible, religious tapes, crosses hung by safety pins on the faded hospital curtains, many cards from her long stay there, religious tracts, flowers from church, and notes from prayer groups.

Throughout her illness her family and friends have encouraged the belief that God would surely cure her because she was such a devoutly religious woman—despite her physician's statements to the contrary. Thus, the air around her deathbed is charged with anger, tension, fear, and growing disbelief.

With her family silently watching, the patient breathes one last shallow breath and—it is finished. Her husband looks up at his daughter and says: "This wasn't supposed to happen." As Emma Hawley died a large part of her family's faith and belief died with her.

This scene is repeated with alarming regularity, not only in situations of serious illness and death but also in the lesser traumas of minor surgery and recoverable illness. It is clear from these and other comments made by patients, visitors, and healthcare workers that contemporary church teaching about death is either grossly misinterpreted or theologically bankrupt.

Perhaps practical matters such as heating the building, paying inflated maintenance costs, or dealing with drugs, divorce, and alcoholism have demanded a higher priority in the church's agenda. Perhaps clergy and others have been poorly prepared to accurately interpret the particular denomination's understanding of these issues. Perhaps in our haste to deny our mortality we gloss over the frightening and painful issues of death and dying, and in doing so have developed a theologically shallow and ultimately dysfunctional system of beliefs to protect and insulate ourselves from the inevitable.

Whatever the reason, contemporary Christian belief about illness and death has been ultimately reduced to a number of trendy slogans. All of us, clergy and laity alike, have used these stock phrases with ourselves and others. Mostly the words have seemed harmless social niceties spoken because we have heard them said before, because they seem to have something to do with church, and because we don't know what else to say. Seldom, however, have we examined the implications of the content of the phrases, much less their effect on the patients and families hearing them from the perspective of the sickbed.

When closely examined, the slogans are seen to be both demanding and disturbing. Each phrase *demands* something on the part of the patient, the family, and God. The person must conform to a certain set of criteria for healing, accept a particular explanation for the event, or behave in a specified manner.

Furthermore, while many persons say that they are trying to console the ill or dying patient or family member, the phrases result only in further disturbing everyone involved. Rather than being helpful, these slogans are a way of shutting down the conversation by glibly presenting a banal answer or solution to understanding the illness. To use them is to convey that the visitor really does not want to talk about what is meaningful to the patient but rather wants to avoid any mention of the fearful issues of uncertainty or death.

The following pronouncements are the most common examples of current American "theology by slogan."

1. God will cure him (her). (Expect a miracle.) Although many people would argue otherwise, this statement has nothing to do with faith. It is, rather, another method of denial and protectiveness. It denies the reality of the patient's pain, illness, discomfort, and dying and so protects the visitor from sharing any of those uncomfortable experiences. Instead of listening to the medical information that is given and making the most of the time left, people offer this theological slogan which serves to insulate and further isolate the patient and family.

The words also demand that the patient make a choice between medicine and faith. Imagine the patient whose doctor has just said he has less than six months to live and is then confronted with his prayer group demanding a cure from God and the patient and the physician. This unnecessary dilemma only increases the sense of confusion and helplessness. It also results in anger and resentment when the members of the family who had expected a miracle are faced with a death for which they were not at all prepared.

In fact, medicine and faith need not be viewed as opposites working toward contrary goals. The first tribal shamans were both priests *and* physicians. The two roles have only recently been separated as disagreements have arisen between science and religion. For the good of the patient and family, it is possible to accept and combine the unique offerings of each perspective into a realistic, prayerful, scientific *and* sacramental approach to illness and death.

2. If you have enough faith, you'll be healed. This often stated slogan assumes that the patient's worsening condition is directly proportional to a lack of faith. Demanding that the patient "try harder" with some internal spiritual resource, the phrase suggests healing is merely the result of extra effort. In fact, the result of such a comment is the creation of a deepening cycle of depression and despair. The patient, dying or in pain, feels responsible for having too little faith to overcome the situation, then feels guilty for that lack, and depressed or angry at the unreasonable demand.

The Gospel information concerning healing is quite different from the popular expression embodied in this statement. Healing in the New Testament has a vastly broader meaning than usually given it, and it happens in a much different manner.

Clergy and physicians are the worst offenders at seeing healing in an extremely narrow context. Usually "healing" when used by either group means physiological change has taken place: the tumor vanishes, the blood pressure returns to normal, the intestinal blockage breaks up. In fact, to hear clergy and physicians talk, the only *acceptable* form of "healing" is this kind of obvious physiological change.

But "healing" is much broader than this myopic, demanding definition. In fact, many things can be healed. Memories can be healed, dreams, disappointments and broken relationships can be healed; anger, resentment, and guilt of a lifetime can be healed; fear of pain, rejection, and judgment can be healed.

And all of this *healing* takes place *during the course of the dying,* so that death and healing, again, are not opposites. Quite the contrary: Death, viewed from this perspective, is a part of that ongoing process of healing which ultimately results in being in "God's nearer presence," where perfect wholeness has occurred.

Sometimes, and only sometimes, bodies are healed also, but that ought to be the *last* goal and understanding of healing, not the first. To see the whole person, as Jesus did, is to view healing in the context of that whole person and not just myopically focus on a required change in the physiological disease process.

It is interesting that this slogan focuses on and demands action on the part of the sick person, when the Biblical evidence is quite the opposite. In nearly every instance of healing, the event has nothing to do with the faith of the sick person. When the centurion comes to Jesus, his servant is not even in sight. When the man's friends lower him down through the roof tiles, we are told that "when Jesus saw *their* faith" the man was healed.

Thus, the healing of sick or dying patients has *nothing* to do with *their own* faith (or lack of it). Biblical evidence points out that healing occurs in the context of the faith of the believing, caring, nurturing *community* surrounding that patient. It is within the context of *these* relationships—the servant's centurion master, the man's concerned friends, the visitors who come to hospitals, whether family or otherwise—that faith and healing interact, not in the individual faith of the sick person. Healing takes place in the context of the community of believers, and that healing may be of past, present or future occurrences. Sometimes it may also be physiological. Often, the form that healing takes is death.

3. *It is God's will.* This covers everything from birth defects to hemorrhoids. It is often alleged to be the faithful person's answer to "Why me?"

Assuming that disease, congenital abnormalities, or self inflicted abuse are somehow the mysterious "will of God" implies that God is responsible for purposely planning these occurrences, usually to further some vague cosmic plan which the sick person is not allowed to question. If this belief is true, then God is as capricious, vindictive, and reprehensible as the diseases and disorders are insidious.

It is theologically inconsistent with the Biblical evidence of the Gospels to believe that God wills or wants people to have disease and sickness. Yet most people would prefer to think that God is the purveyor of pain and disability than to recognize the two major components of illness: personal responsibility and randomness.

We all know that there are certain things we can eat, smoke, drink, and do with our bodies (or not do, such as exercise) to increase the probability that we will be physical and emotional wrecks in 20 to 30 years. And yet, after 20 years of smoking, ingesting the usual American high calorie, high fat, high sugar and cholesterol diet, persons with cardiovascular difficulties suddenly blame their condition on *God's will.* The same argument is used for other stress related, or even genetically related illnesses. In fact, most people would like to relieve themselves of the responsibility for their health and wellness, relegating that chore to expensive, high technology "miracle medicine," and to a God who they hope will rescue them from their own imprudent lifestyles. Thus, when major illness strikes, they drag out God as the culprit.

Similarly, many people would prefer to believe that God plans out illness, distributes it like door prizes at birthday parties, and generally is in control of everyone's destiny. While this rather rigid understanding of God may be comforting for some, it completely ignores the element of randomness in disease. It also ignores free will. Imputing meaning and even intention to illness is a way of refusing to see that, as in many natural occurrences, some people get it and some people don't. Viruses and bacteria and whatever else may be precursors to disease seem to have as much free will to exist at random as the rest of us. Not knowing "why" people get disease (even when they have attempted to stack the odds in their favor through exercise, diet, etc.), many would rather rush to the mysterious will of a dictator-God than to embrace the lifetime of uncertainty that free will implies.

Personal responsibility and free will provide a particular image of God that will be examined in depth later. For further exploration of this complex issue, see the treatise by Leslie Weatherhead entitled, appropriately enough, *The Will of God* where the intentional, circumstantial, and ultimate wills of God are described.

4. There's a reason for everything. The Lord works in strange ways. A corollary of the previous slogan, this one has a slightly different nuance. In addition to assuming God is still playing Trivial Pursuit with your life and inflicting illness to make an unknown and probably unknowable point, there is also an emotional undertone of retribution. It assumes God is out to get you and finally did. It also implies you probably deserved it, and that somewhere, deep down inside, you know what you did to bring about the vindictive disease process with which you are now rightfully plagued.

Although sometimes stated as a message of comfort, the slogan is taken by patients as an affront, and rightly so. Rather than comforting someone who has just had a full-term stillborn, been given the news of an inoperable cancer, or told his arthritis will eventually be crippling, this theological anomaly results in anger, defensiveness, and disbelief.

Once again, Biblical evidence, personal responsibility, and randomness of disease are disavowed in favor of belief in a God who exercises a flawless memory with unmerciful vindictiveness.

5. You have to be strong. A theological injunction particularly common to men, this slogan confuses Jesus with John Wayne. If one is faithful, so the logic goes, one has nothing to fear, nothing about which to be sad, no reason to cry or be depressed or enraged. Patients tell themselves to be strong for their families, and families are strong for the patients. (One very pious older woman said, "Where

there's faith there's no fear. Where there's fear there's no faith."
Great alliteration; terrible theology.)

What this slogan obscures is a conspiracy of denial. It is a denial
of feelings, a denial of medical facts, and a denial of Christ Jesus'
message of support and suffering with us. Hiding behind the model of Christian "strength," patients and families are able to deny
their fear, sadness, and anger. They can ignore the advice of the
physician and nurses to talk about the situation. They can totally
miss the intent of Jesus' presence until it is too late to feel, talk, and
be nurtured.

Contrary to this much practiced bit of popular wisdom, it is not
only "okay" but *recommended* to be "weak" in the face of serious illness. It is desirable to cry, rage, to sink into the depths of depression, to reject, demand, bargain and wish. All these emotions are a
natural part of us, and their expression can be used to increase or
open up communication with God and one another and thus to
strengthen, not diminish, faith.

To repress and deny our thoughts and feelings, even the un-
thinkable ones, is to forget that Christ Jesus exhibited all of these
and more in the Garden of Gethsemane, where he tried to renegotiate his future three times.

6. *You don't die until your number comes up.* This often-heard re-
mark reduces God to the clerk in the deli section of the supermar-
ket. One can imagine God in a white deli apron standing behind
the counter pulling the chain and announcing "Number 103," while
people in hospital beds all over the universe painfully wait, their
ticket stubs clenched in painful, clammy hands.

The function of the slogan is to attempt to understand unexpect-
ed recoveries, spontaneous remissions, and long term "lingering."
The implication is that God personally decides the time of death for
each individual, based on an unknown formula having something
vaguely to do with guilt, suffering, reward, retribution, and, only
occasionally, with mercy.

The experience of caregivers who frequently observe deaths is
quite the opposite. Very often, in fact, people decide their own time
of death. It is not at all uncommon to hear hospital stories of persons who physiologically could have lived for months but one day

decided to quit—and died. Often the death decision relates to a particular date: birthday, wedding anniversary, holiday, or special day of remembrance for that couple or family.

Sometimes the comatose or seriously ill person will wait for the arrival of a particular relative, grandchild, or friend. Thus it is important to keep people informed of what persons are in the room, and who is arriving from out of town.

In the situation of a long, lingering process of dying, the patient may be waiting for "permission" to die. Once the family has verbally expressed to the person that they (the family) will be all right, that they will look after the survivor, and that it is okay to let go, the patient takes a deep sighing breath (of relief?) and dies, sometimes in a matter of minutes.

Especially in the case of close friends or family, people may tend to feel extremely guilty if they are not present at the very moment of death. And yet it is important to remember that patients frequently wait to die until their loved ones are *out of the room*.

Perhaps death is so intimately personal that one wants to do it alone; perhaps separation is so painful that the patient wishes to spare the loved one further anguish; or perhaps they fear the survivor will have to live with the memory of the death scene forever. In any case, from newborn infants to the elderly, one need not be surprised (or feel guilty for not being there) if the patient dies when loved ones are absent.

7. *God took him (her)*. More direct than the previous line, but still presupposing an all-controlling God who capriciously determines our fate, this slogan makes God into a celestial body snatcher, or as one person said, "the great Hoover in the sky," randomly vacuuming people up off the earth. If true, it is no wonder survivors feel frustrated and angry at God. Rather than providing comfort, this statement often results in blame and resentment for God's alleged theft by appropriation.

But the New Testament has no place for a God who randomly and inexplicably "takes" people away from the ones they love. We see there instead a very different picture of trust and nurturing. Rather than "taking" the seriously ill person in some mysterious way we are not to question, the God of the Gospels is presented as one who welcomes and *accepts us with open arms when our bodies quit working.* God, then, is not the killer of infants, the murderer of the elderly, the destroyer of lives. God, to the contrary, is the welcomer of spent bodies, the comforter of mourners, the lover of all souls.

Whether survivors follow the image of an accepting, welcoming God or a controlling, taking God makes a great deal of difference in how they will grieve and how much they will continue to turn to God for support in the future.

8. Time heals all wounds. While purporting to express sympathetic understanding, this statement actually implies that sickness is abnormal and self-indulgent; it subtly demands that patients hurry up and get well, or that families "deal with" the illness or loss quickly, as though the mere passage of time guaranteed healing. To be told "time heals all wounds" is to be judged guilty of psychological malingering and urged to move on and be over the death, since an adequate amount of time has presumably passed.

The truth is that time itself does *not heal anything.* In fact, time makes it worse—always. Especially during the first year (and often into the second and third) following the death of a loved one, the passage of time will exacerbate the pain and loneliness by daily verifying the reality of the loss. With the passage of birthdays, anniversaries, holidays, special days for the couple, and the anniversary of the death and the funeral, the feelings of loss and grief are made *worse,* not easier. Indeed there are some losses over which we may grieve our entire lives, and that process is perfectly normal.

It is also true that people will handle grieving (whether anticipatory grieving by the patient and family at the time of diagnosis and during the illness, or on the part of the survivors following the death) the same way they handle other major problems in their lives—at their *own* pace and following their *own* style of managing and coping. To be urged to comply with another person's manner and time schedule is both insensitive and unrealistic. Such a demand has more to do with the discomfort of the onlooker than it does with real concern for the person experiencing the loss.

Christian theology never equates time with healing. Rather, the stories and parables throughout the New Testament indicate that *repentance, faith, love, forgiveness, relationships,* and *trust* heal, not time. It is far more helpful to support these experiences than to demand a change in sad or grieving behavior in order to alleviate our own discomfort.

It is important to remember that all of these slogans are attempts to use ideas thought to be based on Christian theology to come to terms with the realities of sickness, healing, and death. They are not, in fact, examples of Christian theology, but rather are statements of an American civil religion which presupposes an all-controlling, all-responsible, capricious, and punitive God. As such they function to reinforce an optimistic worldview of a national God who rewards good (our country) and punishes evil (our enemies) and who sees illness either as a logical punishment for real or imagined wrongdoing or as part of a plan of an individual Manifest Destiny.

A major issue raised by the examination of these slogans is the nature of good and evil. The church also has taught for centuries that good is rewarded and evil punished. Yet anyone old enough to read the headlines of their local newspaper knows that is untrue. What, then, is the value in being "good?" What ought we to be teaching our children about the real nature of good and evil? How will we understand these ideas ourselves and how will we relate them to illness and death? It is clear that much more study and education need to be done at the local church level in order to relieve the confusion and disruption caused by the poor theologizing characterized in the slogans listed above.

One of the ways to approach this discussion is through the two major (and opposing) views of God. The first posits an *active God in a responsive universe.* This belief system sees God as omniscient, omnipresent, all-powerful and in total control, while the rest of the universe (including illness and death) merely responds to God's command.

The second view assumes a *responsive God in an active universe.* This system sees the universe actively, freely going about its natural business of building up and breaking down, living and dying, while God, supporting the free will of natural and human law, seeks to respond to that activity. This belief structure finds God not sending or controlling disease, but rather supporting and upholding those afflicted with illness—*suffering with them*, and grieving with them and their survivors.

In their need to combat the feelings of helplessness and loss of control, it is understandable that many people choose to believe in an active God who is totally in charge. But, as Weatherhead says in *The Will of God:* "There is ultimately no comfort in a lie." The slogans, therefore, and the God they presuppose, will ultimately prove shallow and unfulfilling. They are also inconsistent with the image presented in the New Testament of a loving, forgiving, merciful God who sees humankind as co-creators. It is this God who, as shown in Christ Jesus, suffers *with* us, feels helpless *with* us, *shares with us* our sense of being out of control. It is only this God who can affirm *both* our living *and* our dying.

FREEDOM

They made a coffin for me
Then they put me in a box
They laid me on silk pillows
To keep me from all shocks.
They told me to rest quietly
And not disturb their peace:
If I was a good girl
One day I'd get release.

They nailed the lid upon me,
Put a hammer in my hands
And I hit the final nail in
As propriety demands.

Then, Lord, you came and broke in,
Wrenched the lid from off the box,
Gave bread to my enfeebled frame,
Blood to revive my stock.

You grasped my hands in your hands,
Threw the pillows far away,
Said, "Kathryn, dare you follow
Into the light of day?

Your eyes will be no use to you,
The radiance is so bright;
But if you follow close to me
You need not fear the light."

I left the box behind me,
Forgot propriety's demands,
Stumbled gladly into freedom
Holding you with both my hands.

Then today I was fainthearted,
I wanted to see ahead.
I took my hands from you, my Lord,
Looked out of the light instead.

I saw a wasted desert,
No water anywhere,
Corpses, coffins with silk pillows—
That's all was growing there.

That graveyard's where I could be
But it's what I've left behind.
Accept these hands again, my Lord,
Let your light make me blind.

K.M.V. Morfey

8

Death and Spirituality

The previous two chapters have indicated that we who say we are Christians are quite reluctant to make death planning decisions for ourselves or others. Though we claim to know something of dying as the central core of our belief, our slogan approach to theology reveals a death-denying orientation based more on civil religion than on traditional Biblical thought. Following directly from these situations is the formation of a spirituality that also denies, fears and avoids acknowledgment of finitude and death.

One of the ways that spiritual system begins to develop is by the use in our culture of carefully chosen euphemisms to insulate ourselves from the reality of death. Phrases like *passed away, gone, lost, going down the tubes, cashed in his chips,* or *bit the dust* are common expressions for death. A favorite healthcare euphemism is *expired.* Library cards and parking meters expire. *People* die.

Sometimes just before death we say the person is: *on his last leg, ready to go, hanging on by a thread, circling the drain, preparing for the celestial discharge,* or *packing it in.* Even the Roman Catholic church has changed its theology, naming "the sacrament of the sick" what used to be known as "last rites" or "extreme unction."

We also portray our relationship with death in *military* language and metaphors. We describe patients as having *fought the good fight, lost the battle, gave up the ship/ghost,* or *surrendered to their fate.* We bring in the *troops, combat* illness and disease, *triage* patients, *allocate* resources. Patients are seen and described as *victims* of heart attacks, cancer and stroke. Germs *invade* the body; physicians and nurses *feel defeated* when they do not *successfully overcome* a disease. This military imagery sets up yet another good/bad dichotomy where death is never an acceptable outcome.

In an attempt to lessen the fear of death and further deny its reality, we tell some wonderful jokes about the afterlife. To illustrate just how many are in our common memory, it is necessary only to list a few of the punch lines: *Oh, that's just God, he likes to pretend he's a doctor; Be quiet, they think they're the only ones up here; Oh, that's just God, he likes to pretend he's Tom Landry; The good news is there's baseball in heaven, the bad news is you're scheduled to pitch tomorrow.*

Our language describing illness, dying, and afterlife accurately reflects a mirror image of our spiritual belief about death. And the image is that death is bad, the evil enemy, wrong, unacceptable, and unjust.

As we have seen, the church seems to have exacerbated and supported this denial by consistently offering an inadequately defined theology, resulting in the previously presented cliches. The euphemisms, military language, jokes, and theological slogans are further evidence of the shallowness, misunderstanding, and fear surrounding death and dying. And those characteristics show themselves in contemporary Christian spirituality.

How might we, then, approach death so as to better integrate it into our spiritual journeys? The following ideas may be helpful as guidelines.

Death as daily process   That we each die a little bit every day is not only metaphorically true, it is indeed *physiologically* true. Each day we destroy millions of cells, most of which are replenished in our systems with new ones. In addition, the natural, normal aging process accelerates as our bodies expand, grow, and work their way toward atrophy, deterioration, and death. Because we are looking from the inside out we usually do not see this daily process; it only becomes evident after the passage of time, or when seeing our photographs compared with those of a few years ago. Daily physiological death is necessary in order for new cells to generate and take over. It is likewise ultimately necessary for us (as whole bodies, collections of cells) to die so that our children and grand-children can take over what we have left behind.

It is also true that we die a little each day *psychologically*. As we take in new data about who we are, about the way we see ourselves and others, about our past, our parents and growing up, it is neces-sary, if we are to allow ourselves to mature, to let the old images of ourselves die. Likewise, old images of our parents, our families, and our children must also die and be replaced by new ones if we are to see these people as who they are now. This psychological death is largely out of our immediate awareness although we get glimpses of it through new dreams and new relationships.

We also die *spiritually* every day. Just as psychological and phys-iological processes continue to evolve within us, so spiritual growth can only take place if we allow our images of God to die daily, along with imagesof ourselves in relationship to God. If we do *not* let them die, rigor mortis sets in. We find ourselves defending rigid spiritual beliefs, unchangeable ideas of God and the world, with an unwillingness to let God's new words break into us because we are so comfortably surrounded by ancient beliefs and images.

The biblical witness of Jesus is clear on the fact that God does not wish us to live forever under the same beliefs, rituals, and images of ourselves and God. As God dies daily—changes, renews, heals, overturns—so we must also as made in God's image. To accept our task of dying daily is to begin to see death as a normal part of daily living.

Hospital and other institutional caregivers who are present at the bedsides of hundreds of dying patients know from experience (often contrary to their own belief at first) that death is normal, nat-ural, expected, and often welcomed at any age. As they see people die, watching the lines drop from their faces, watching them relax, be calm and at peace for the first time in months, death loses its horror and fearsomeness and becomes as natural and acceptable as any other part of our life's journey.

Death as daily process—physiologically, psychologically, and spiritually—is the first step toward realistic Christian spirituality.

Death as letting go   Jesus was constantly telling people to die, to be reborn, and to let go of things. He indicated that they indeed could not be reborn, know the kingdom of heaven, or have peace until they *did* let go.

It's as though Jesus knew the stress and energy we use, or that consumes us, in our desperate attempts to control, to hold on, and to understand. He understood that that same energy could be used for other, more significant endeavors in the building of the kingdom. And he understood from his own experience that it was in the letting go that the death and new life were able to occur, and *only* in that experience.

It was only after the tables were overturned that the temple could be a place of healing. The image is the same for us: unless we are willing to have our carefully placed, comfortable tables that are secure and known overturned, healing cannot and will not occur in our lives.

It was only after letting go in the Garden of Gethsemane that Jesus was able to feel peaceful and face his death realistically. The image is the same for us: unless we are willing to desperately argue, to wrestle and grapple with our God and then to let go, we will never know the peace that "passes all understanding."

It was only after crying out in anguish and despair, and questioning on the cross that Jesus again let go and *risked* resurrection. The image is the same for us: unless we are willing to question, cry out, and, once again, let go and die, we will never know the present meaning of resurrection in our lives.

The images are clear: We are called by God to let go. Some of the things we are encouraged to let go of are:

Parents   Jesus was speaking plainly and psychologically when he said "Unless you forsake father, mother, sister, brother for my sake you will not know the kingdom of heaven." It is indeed true that unless we let go of images of our parents and the family we grew up in, unless we relinquish them and stop blaming that environment and those people for our present day difficulties, we will never be free to grow in the here and now.

We will never be free to know the kingdom of heaven because we are too (literally) damned busy hanging on to the past, hanging on to grudges, to unfinished business that can never be done, to mistakes we made, to things we said or didn't say or that were said and done to us. Unless we literally let go of the image of parents and/or family in our heads, we will not know the kingdom of heaven. It is crucial to our spirituality and our spiritual journey that we relinquish those images and allow those feelings to die.

Children The same statement is equally true concerning our children. We do not own them and they do not own us. If we would allow ourselves to see them as separate people rather than as "the children," some incredible changes would immediately occur in our relationships, in our expectations, in our demands, and in our exchange of feelings with each other. If we were willing to drop the bonds, the expectations, the assumptions about their and our behavior regarding wishes for love and attention, then each of us would be free to give and get those things if we so chose, not because they were demanded. When Jesus said "Let the little children come to me," he meant yours and mine. If they belong to God (which they do, as do we all) then we exist in new relationships. It is important to our spirituality that we also let go of our children from birth.

The world Jesus said "Be not conformed to this world." As Christians we are daily confronted with advertising messages on how to be, who to be, how much to spend. We are told repeatedly how much popularity, power, and prestige our money and influence can buy us. We are warned in contrast by Jesus to be careful with these powerful objects.

We are also told the world is not a forbidden or foreboding place, that there are pleasures abounding here and we are to enjoy them as much as possible, smelling the flowers along the way, loving and being loved, hugging, being sexual, sensual, sensitive and caring, wallowing in the simple luxuries God has provided for us in this world.

It is no wonder then that we get so attached to our existence here and to the people with us. Hospice and hospital caregivers daily witness dying patients fearing leaving this world, who are angry at leaving these pleasures and pains behind and leaving behind the ones they love and have loved for many, many years. Such attachment is deep and painful to break off.

And yet the message is clear: "Be not conformed to this world." We are clearly told that the world is larger than we see it now; that there is more to life than the physicalness we experience here and now. Death is a passage from life to life, as are childhood, adolescence, adulthood, and old age.

Letting go of the world is the beginning of coming to terms with our unrealistic images of power and control. Letting go of the world, detaching ourselves from it ultimately while working in it penultimately, is a crucial part of developing a daily spiritual life.

God   This is perhaps the most difficult death of all. And yet, if we are to find God we must let go of him/her/it or however we see and use God. It is not only true that "They who save their lives will lose them and they who lose their lives for my sake will save them." It is also true that whoever hangs on to God will never find God and whoever lets go of God, who dies to God and lets God die to him or her, only that person will ever know God as God is.

Death as letting go of God means letting go of God as always in control; God as ultimate punisher and demander; God as made in the image of our father or mother, or God as the anthropomorphic image of ourselves. It is to let go of God as the cosmic vending machine into whom we put our fifty cent prayers and out of whom come the candy answers and solutions. It is to let go of God as the cosmic insurance policy guaranteeing that life is ultimately fair and will turn out all right; God as the defender of whatever our current cause happens to be and vanquisher of national and international foes. Indeed, letting go of God means letting go of God as the ultimate denier of death and accepting the fact that God is as helpless as we are.

Dietrich Bonhoeffer in his *Ethics* describes this image of death as the letting go of God:

> The God who makes us live in this world without using him as a working hypothesis is the God before whom we are ever standing. Before God and with him we live without God. God allows himself to be edged out of the world and on to the cross. God is weak and powerless in the world, and that is exactly the way, the only way, in which he can be with us and help us. It is not by his omnipotence that Christ helps us, but by his weakness and suffering.

This is the decisive difference between Christianity and all religions. Man's religiosity makes him look in his distress to the power of God in the world; he uses God as a Deus ex machina. The Bible however directs him to the powerlessness and suffering of God; only a suffering God can help.

Death as letting go means letting go of the God we currently know and allowing God to witness to us out of weakness in the world with us, by us and for us.

Death is a powerful paradigm for our spirituality. Until we come to terms with our own death we will not have come to terms with our life, alone, and alone with God.

IV
SURVIVING DEATH

9

Grief Tasks

Just as there are no "stages" of dying, so there are no such easily identifiable categories of grieving. Elisabeth Kübler-Ross did provide assistance in understanding the behaviors that a dying patient is likely to exhibit with five phases: denial, anger, bargaining, depression and acceptance. But it does a severe disservice to a dying patient and family to label their reactions merely for the purpose of pigeonholing them, demanding they fit into these neat boxes and move through them sequentially.

The phases are, in fact, seldom seen in a regular sequential order. The patient may feel angry one day, depressed the next, and denying the next. Or the time frame for these reactions may be a matter of hours or minutes. The categories, therefore, are better understood as "tasks" to be performed in no particular time or pattern, with no moral judgment determining which phases are "good" and which are "bad."

These same guidelines can be applied to the process of grieving. While many persons have described "stages" of grief, it is important both to survivors and the people interacting with them not to categorize or demand that they move through these phases in a particular sequence. Rather, these reactions, too, must be seen as "tasks" to be performed or behaviors that are likely to be evidenced as the survivor responds to the death.

One of the best models for describing grief reactions is that of Colin Murray Parkes. In his book, *Bereavement—A Study of Grief in Adult Life*, Parkes, borrowing somewhat from Kübler-Ross, sets forth five "stages" of grieving, complete with suggested time frames. With the disclaimers mentioned above about sequence and stages, the Parkes model is a useful way to understand the tasks of grieving.

1. Alarm/shock The initial reaction to the death, whether sudden or expected is the same. As one emotionally distraught family member said when her mother had taken a last breath: "You get prepared but you never get ready." Even when funeral plans have been made, the will is in order, and a Living Will has enabled the patient's wishes to be honored, there is something about the finality of the actual death that is always disturbing at a deep level for the survivors. The tears, the wailing, and the stoicism reflected by different cultures all indicate both the shock of the loss of the patient, and the alarm of the realization that the survivor will also one day die.

A common occurrence during this period is sleep disturbance. The survivor may sleep constantly or not at all. Especially after a long illness, the person may be so physically exhausted that extra sleep time is needed to recuperate. Feelings of "weariness" and "numbness" are pervasive. As the person begins to work through the events surrounding the death, time is needed for the body to process those events and make them part of the present understanding and mind set. This "processing" often takes the form of lying in bed for hours on end, thinking, staring at the ceiling, remembering, and feeling. Survivors for whom the normal routine was early rising followed by a regimen of work or caretaking or hospital visits may think they are "cracking up," "falling apart," or "going crazy" because of their weariness or inordinate need for rest.

Likewise, people who were once sound sleepers now find themselves unable to make it through the night without waking every couple or three hours, only to have difficulty getting back to sleep. Dreams, flashbacks to the scene of the death and the funeral, concerns about the future (financial, social, health), as well as the physical difference of not having the person in the house or in the bed all combine to prevent sleep and rest.

While Parkes believes that this reaction occurs mainly in the first two weeks after the death, it is entirely possible for the survivor to awaken on a birthday, anniversary, or holiday many months hence and have the same feelings of alarm and shock. The important thing is to know that these feelings, along with the sleep disturbances, are common to persons who have experienced a death.

2. *Searching* After the initial shock has passed somewhat, a period of searching ensues. This is a time of pining, of intense yearning for the dead person, and of continuing to act as if that person were still alive. There is a part of the survivor that will not believe the death has happened, protesting the event by still going through the old behavior patterns as though the loved one was there.

The survivor may think of something to tell the person, pick up the phone and dial the first few digits of the number, then put the receiver down, realizing that there will be no one there. The survivor may start to write the person a note, barely getting through the name before the paper is wadded up and thrown away. Pulling into the driveway after a busy day at work, the survivor may look forward to telling the loved one some particular incident of importance, imagining the person to be fixing dinner in the kitchen, then suddenly remember that there will be no one there to tell. This part of the search is the expectation that the person will continue to be present in the old patterns of relating.

Another part of this task is the search around town for the missing person. As the survivor continues on with his or her life, frequenting the same places for shopping, religious services, entertainment, study, and relaxation, she or he keeps one eye open to spot the loved one, imagining the person will be physically or spiritually present there. It is not unusual during this time for survivors to report hearing, seeing, or smelling the scent of the loved one.

Frequently the survivor will return to the hospital or nursing unit for a brief visit. While ostensibly this visit is to thank the nurses or staff for their good care and to bring them some gift of flowers, fruit, or candy, the survivor invariably wants to stop by the room where the loved one died. There is something very therapeutic or completing about the experience, painful as it usually is. It is as though the survivor is searching, but at the same time validating that the loved one really is no longer there. Friends or staff members can help by understanding this need, and by offering to accompany the survivor on this painful journey.

Again, although Parkes places this period at four to six weeks after the first, the search continues off and on for many people for years and years to come.

3. _Mitigation_ This task, according to Parkes, occurs about the third or fourth month, when the searching begins to come to an end. The pain starts to ease and the protest lessens somewhat. No longer does the survivor think of what to say to the person while driving home. No notes are begun. The phone is not dialed. The results of the search are becoming more obvious and reluctantly acceptable.

Understandably, this is a time of depression and deep despair. Coming to terms with the emptiness is a painful and difficult task. As Parkes quite beautifully describes it, this period is the one in which "presence changes to memory." The survivor begins to have an image of the loved one no longer as present, but as past. The expectation that the person will be nearby diminishes and is replaced by the resignation to find that person only in memories.

This task frequently involves the processing of grieving dreams. Often the following sequence of dreams has been reported:

A. The survivor sees the loved one as dead, in a casket, on a slab, lying down, with no affect, no movement, no color in the lifeless body. There is no interaction between the two in this set of dreams.

B. The survivor sees the loved one as dead, but the loved one is sitting up and talking with the survivor. There is still no affect, no color or life in the body, but there is interaction. Often the talk is purely factual, rather than emotional.

C. The survivor is home alone in a room in the house (or elsewhere) and suddenly becomes aware that someone has entered the room. Turning around, the survivor is shocked to see it is the dead loved one. This time, the loved one is clearly alive, color and affect are seen in the body, and conversation takes place as though it picked up where they left off before the death. The survivor feels stunned, confused, and often worried about explaining events that have taken place since the loved one's death.

D. The survivor goes to visit the loved one in another place (house, apartment, city, etc.) The loved one is usually happy, smiling, pleasant and the scene is sunny and attractive. This scenario usually signals the end of the sequence. Dreams from here out may be sporadic, relating to specific instances in the growth or experience of the survivor.

Frequently (especially in the third set of dreams) these experiences are so real and powerful that the survivor will awaken feeling confused about whether or not the loved one is really there.

Keeping a journal can be an important method for working through the task of mitigation. Recording the dreams, the survivor will begin to see a pattern of progression from images of death to images of health, both for the survivor and the loved one. Writing a dialogue with the dead person can be very helpful in working out whatever unfinished business there might be to complete. Composing a letter, saying the unsaid things, stating unstated feelings and thoughts can be useful. Sometimes, going to the grave (if there is one) and talking to the person can help to work through the depression and despair.

Whatever methods are chosen, friends are an indispensable part of this task. They need to be there to listen, support, and hold the survivor as the pain and presence move toward mitigation and memory.

4. *Anger/guilt*   The fifth and sixth month, following the Parkes model, are filled with emotional turmoil. This is a period of the "what ifs:"

• "What if we'd have caught it earlier?"

"What if he'd gone to the doctor like I asked him to six months ago?"

• "What if she'd had one more chemotherapy treatment?"

• "What if I'd have spent more time with him?"

• "What if a different doctor had seen her?"

The survivor is torn with guilt about things that were done and things that were not done, things that were and were not said, or thought, or imagined. Feelings of anger surface from deep within the grieving person and are aimed at the caregivers, the family, friends, God, the survivor—and frequently at the dead person. Then the survivor feels guilty for feeling angry at those persons, especially the loved one. Such feelings need to be affirmed as acceptable, understandable, and necessary.

Anger and guilt are overwhelming as the person goes on with life without the dead person. There is anger about socializing alone, guilt about seeing other people; anger at others who get to go on together, guilt about resenting their happiness, or at least their companionship. There is anger at being in the situation of having sustained a loss that will never be retrieved, and guilt about coming to terms with it.

Once again, knowing that the feelings are to be expected can help obviate the fear that the survivor is the only person who ever experienced them. Talking to others in a bereavement group or having coffee with the hospital chaplain, social worker, or Hospice volunteer can allow the survivor to ventilate with someone who is not going to give advice, but rather listen with understanding and confidence.

5. Identity/recovery Eventually (Parkes says during the last six months of the first year), the survivor begins to move back into social events, religious and community activities, and work or other daily routines. New patterns are formed, new relationships developed, and a new identity begins to emerge based on parts of the old and parts of the new self.

This is a very difficult, tender, and vulnerable time. The survivor is testing out new behaviors, or rather using old ones and updating them with new experiences. He or she, therefore, may feel extremely tentative during this period, and may need sustaining without pushing, understanding without judgment.

The survivor may seek out different kinds of persons entirely, or may jump too quickly into a relationship for which she or he seems unready. (See Chapters 10 and 11.) Going to a movie, out to dinner, or to a social gathering may seem like a good idea at the time, but turn out to be too overwhelming once there. Friends can allow grieving persons the freedom to change their mind at the last minute, or to leave when they feel the need, regardless of the hour or circumstance.

With good friends supporting and affirming the survivor during this time, a new identity will develop that will integrate the dead loved one into the pattern of the person's past. Strengthening that identity and developing it further will very likely take the rest of life to complete.

It is important to reiterate that these tasks are not necessarily sequential. They may be performed and felt in any order and at any time. The original in-depth grief studies conducted following the Cocoanut Grove fire in Boston in 1942 concluded that if survivors were still having grief reactions after *six weeks,* then their response was dysfunctional and they needed psychiatric support. Later studies in the 1960s found that *six months* were needed to *complete* the grieving process. The Parkes model, written in the mid 1970s, suggests a *one year* time frame in which to have all the problems neatly wrapped up and finished. At a recent Hospice symposium, psychologists proposed *two to three years* as a more reasonable period for resolution of grief.

The truth is that people handle grief the same way they handle every other major difficulty in their lives. There is no designated time frame within which survivors *must* resolve their grieving. Whether assertive or passive, with emotions or stoicism, resignation or remorse, they will grieve according to who they are and what works best for them—and they will do it *at their own speed.*

Furthermore, the use of medical imagery is inappropriate for any discussion of grief. While Parkes is accurate in suggesting the formation of new aspects of *identity,* the use of the word "recovery" is misleading and inaccurate. We do not recover from the death of a loved one. In fact, we *never recover* from that death in the same way we recover from an illness or broken limb. It will always be a part of us—*always*—and to suggest otherwise is unrealistically and harshly to imply that we somehow "get over" the feelings about the event or stop experiencing painful reminiscences of the loved one or the death.

A much more accurate metaphor is represented in the old Carole King song "Tapestry."

> My life has been a tapestry of rich and royal hue
> An everlasting vision of the everchanging view
> A wondrous woven magic in bits of blue and gold
> A tapestry to feel and see, impossible to hold.

In fact our lives are "tapestries," and the death of a loved one is a ripping, gaping, bleeding hole in the very midst of that tapestry of our life. How, then, is the tapestry _rewoven?_ It does not, with the mere passage of time, magically pull itself back together. Rather, it is rewoven only with the initiative, energy, and strength of the survivor reaching in and grasping the torn ends of threads, painfully pulling them back and tying them together. And it is rewoven only with those persons _around_ the survivor cutting threads from their _own_ tapestries and bringing them to the survivor, with love and support and caring and tears and strength, helping to further tie the threads and fill in that gaping hole.

So, eventually, the tapestry is _rewoven_. But that "glitch" is always there, the roughness of that reweaving is, and always will be, apparent. In fact it may be twenty years from now, as the survivor reviews the tapestry of his or her life, or is in a particular setting, or hears a song on the radio, or remembers a special day of the month, that the rewoven seam is seen and felt again, and the survivor remembers and cries, or feels sad, or is touched by the love and caring expressed by those whose threads are apparent there—and that is perfectly normal. We do not _recover_ from a death, but, when we allow others to help, we can _reweave_ our tapestry, which may include continuing to grieve from time to time in varying degrees of intensity for the rest of our lives.

Many people want to know how to identify "abnormal" grieving. Obviously bizarre behavior that is out of character for the survivor is relatively easy to recognize. But less blatantly, if it seems clear that the emotional intensity of the survivor is consistently getting in the way of regular patterns of functioning (shopping, eating, work, health), then additional support in the form of counseling or medication could well be in order.

In any case, understanding the framework of grieving is useful both to survivors and their support system. It is only as these two work together that resolution and healing may occur.

10

Sex After Death

Your lover has died. The person you dreamed with, for however long a time, is no longer there to dream with you. The person you shared space with, no matter how big or small, is no longer there to rattle around the house, bother you with tasks or questions, play and laugh with and share secrets and argue and talk with anymore. The person you crawled into bed with late at night and held close and stroked gently and wanted to touch and hold you is gone. The one you snuggled with deep under blankets in the cold sheets of winter and wrestled with in the sweat of summer under ceiling fans and nibbled and kissed and explored, sometimes with passion, sometimes with duty, has suddenly vanished.

The bed, whether double, queen or king, is gigantically vacant. It is as empty as the rest of your life without the one you loved.

Death of a lover is one of those things that is not supposed to happen. It happens in *Love Story* and it happens in the daytime soaps, but it is not part of the script we write for ourselves. It is, indeed, so far from our consciousness that when it does occur we are shocked, devastated, and indelibly changed for the rest of our lives.

While many books and articles are written on grief and bereavement, they seldom deal with the delicate and intensely personal issue of the survivor's need for sexuality and intimacy after death. People who consider themselves friends may jokingly ask "How's your love life?" but, as with grief in general, few seriously approach the subject due to their own discomfort. Survivors are then left with a plethora of questions, feelings, demands, and needs that go unanswered in a society content to focus itself on life and youth; a society where death is consistently denied, as are the needs of those who have experienced it.

The following examination of sex after death is, first of all, meant to provide information for survivors. By discussing common experiences reported by persons who have had a lover die, a picture of usual responses and normally expected tasks will gradually emerge to offer guidelines for this most singular kind of bereavement.

This information may be helpful not only to those who have experienced the loss of a lover. Those who are friends of the bereaved also may gain insight into how they can be more supportive to the survivor and be better prepared when their own lover dies. The guidelines will also be useful to persons who have experienced the death of *anyone* close to them. With the death of a child, parent, close friend, or even co-worker, many of the responses are identical in terms of sexual needs, feelings, and behavior on the part of the survivor.

Although a direction may be seen in the pattern of the descriptions, they are *not* meant to be sequential. For example, while one might assume that "recovery" from the death would begin with loss of libido and end with acceptance of nurturing, the truth is that loss of libido may occur repeatedly and in no particular "order" in the coping process. Similarly, acceptance of nurturing may begin the day after the death and ebb and flow as the survivor accomplishes the other tasks of mourning.

There may be some raised eyebrows at the use of the word "lover." It is an emotionally loaded term because it implies strong, usually sexual, feelings, and is not as definitive or exclusive as the word "spouse." But "lover" is purposely meant here to be *inclu-sive. It can (depending on the reader) mean "spouse," "love," "partner," "friend," or "lover" in the usual sense.

Likewise, in the pages that follow, the term "sexuality" is used because it is the most obvious form of interaction. But one could also read "intimacy" for "sexuality," and be even more inclusive in understanding the dilemmas of vulnerability, openness, and closeness faced by those surviving death.

Feelings of intimacy do not die with the spouse or lover's death, though (as we will see) some temporary abatement will occur. Survivors will continue to be sexually active or intimate in some manner. Initially, and often permanently, this behavior will occur outside of marriage. (Often there are quite reasonable legal, insurance, property, medical, or emotional reasons for this.) The worst that may be said, morally, about this is that it is unfortunate. While marriage may be the desired goal, it is grossly unrealistic to demand it as a requirement for survivors. To do so is to be rigidly legalistic, unforgiving, and unmercifully critical.

The issues discussed are behaviors and episodes that usually occur in the journey following the loss of a love. As with the discussion of death and grieving above, they are to be seen as tasks to be experienced rather than an orderly plan to "overcome" the loss. Likewise, they are not meant to be construed as right or wrong ways to feel, think, or behave. There is no proper or correct way to react to such an experience. There are only the ways that we *do* react, and the following are descriptions of those behaviors.

As survivors slowly make their way through the days following the death, they can expect these events to occur:

1. *Loss of libido* While most people are prepared for the emotional turmoil and exhaustion of grief, they are never told that grief is incredibly physically draining as well. The combination of both the physical and emotional elements logically leads to a diminishment of sexual interest and ability.

Lying in bed for hours at a time, gazing at the ceiling, remembering, sorting out thoughts and plans, all one thinks about is rest from the tasks ahead. Sex is not a high priority when there are so many other things to be done: bills to be corrected and paid, clothes to be donated, business affairs to be settled, children to be tended, employment to be continued or found. Often sex is seen as one more time consuming thing that, fortunately, can be put off a while longer while one uses the available energy to solve the other problems at hand.

People frequently report feeling "numb from the neck down" as depression and sadness drain sensitivity from the skin, and desire is replaced with disinterest. Even sexual dreams end without a climax, accentuating the sense of emptiness, the loss of self worth and desirability.

Often one behaves sexually and otherwise as though the lover is still around, even long after the lover's death. Whether the issue is spending money on a new outfit or observing a potential sex partner, the resulting feeling is one of overwhelming guilt for "cheating" on the loved one or "disrespecting" his or her memory. It is easier not to have sexual stirrings than to have them crushed by the weight of self doubt and guilt.

Early post-death sexual experiences are often reported to be physically or emotionally painful and confusing, fraught with diametrically opposed feelings, and a sense of panic or fear. After one or two such experiences, loss of libido seems a welcome relief.

An underlying issue here is powerlessness. The death of a lover leaves the survivor stranded, alone, powerless to change the situation or to bring the person back. The survivor is overwhelmed, not only with physical tasks to perform, but also with an emotional reshuffling of expectations, plans, and feelings. The result is a sense of helplessness and powerlessness with obvious sexual ramifications.

Eventually, as plans get changed, business is put in order, and immediate decisions are accomplished, the gradual sense of reorganization and control will begin to result in the return of sexual desires, at least temporarily.

2. Sex as searching "Starting over" is a misnomer. Nobody starts over; rather, they continue from where they left off. No one can undo the experiences of the relationship leading up to the time of the lover's death. But an interesting psychological phenomenon commonly reported by survivors is a kind of regression back to the time before sex began with the former partner.

If, for instance, the relationship dates back to one's early twenties, one may suddenly feel as if one is in one's late teens again sexually: uncertain, untried, unsure. It is as though the death somehow wipes out the sexual maturity and experience that occurred during the time of the relationship with the lover and the person is "back to square one again." It is natural, then, to imagine the survivor would search for another partner to renew and continue that lost experience.

However, as one almost "shops" for a replacement during the initial time following the death, the search encounters major impediments. Loss of libido and severe mood swings, from passionate to disinterested, often leave the survivor confused, frustrated, and angry about sexual experiences, with a similar effect on new partners. Sex becomes a perfunctory chore in the search to take up the lonely space that seems never able to be filled.

In fact, many people report that sex makes the loss worse. Flashbacks are commonplace occurrences. In the midst of intimacy or intercourse with a new partner, one's mind races to comparisons with or memories of the dead lover. Lying together afterwards engenders tender feelings of previously happy moments. Whether the sexual experience with the former partner was good or bad, sex now is a constant reminder of that loss, of the lack of what one had, of the pain of the death.

Often this searching is a time of mechanical difficulties during sex: impotence, lack of lubrication, vaginismus, premature (or no) ejaculation. Such experiences only exacerbate the absence of the lover and leave the survivor feeling more despair. It is important to remember that this time, like the time of libido loss, is temporary. With further experiences and the rebuilding of one's sense of self worth, the mechanical and emotional impediments begin to dissipate, even though memories may still blindside the survivor from time to time.

3. Sex as distraction The grieving process is intensely time-consuming. The survivor dwells for moments, hours, even days on the memory of the dead lover, reviewing experiences, wondering about the death and what he or she might have done to prevent or alter it, still hoping for a sign of communication. To help assuage these thoughts, sexual activity is often a strong distraction. It takes one's mind off the past and demands attention powerfully to the present. It helps pass the time, even if one is merely "going through the motions" with a new partner.

With the body feeling generally numb and unresponsive to any outside stimuli, one's sexuality seems to be in neutral. Severe depression and grieving dreams (sometimes sexual ones) further decrease the desire for sexual intimacy with anyone. But even a few sexual contacts may also re-awaken the survivor to the powerful potential of this most distracting and potentially healing pastime.

Recreational sex is frequently a sign of some forward progress on the part of the survivor. If indiscriminate, it can be an indication of the searching process or a behavioral expression of anger. But if sex is pursued for its playfulness and distracting quality, it can be a sign of the beginning of recovery. As the survivor deals more realistically with the loss, he or she is better able to reach out and do what is pleasurable, even if it is only momentarily distracting. The distraction may also develop into new bonding relationships, though this is unlikely in the early months of grieving a lover.

4. Sex as anger   As most people know, anger is a perfectly normal, even healthy, response to death. One has angry feelings at oneself for things done and not done; at the caregivers (physicians, hospital staff, family members) who looked after the loved one; at the pressure from others to be over the grieving; even at the lover for dying and leaving. Often this anger will be expressed sexually.

Indiscriminate sex with multiple partners (as mentioned above) can be a way of striking back at men or women for the loss, or a way to defiantly prove one is still "okay." It can be an angry form of flailing about with no direction, recoiling from the devastation of the death, putting oneself at high risk for disease and even one's own death. Many people report "having sex with a vengeance" as though the kind and number of partners provides a means for getting back at the dead person, or for punishing oneself for guilt about things done or not done, said or not said concerning that death.

Sometimes the anger is directed at the new partner when the survivor realigns too quickly or seeks a replacement for the dead lover. The otherwise normal anger is turned inward to become self punishing or outward to physical or emotional harm to others. Hurtful or violent sexual interactions are expressions of this hostile response to the loss.

Possibly the most difficult kind of anger to experience or express is anger about the situation. The lover's death was not in the scenario the two had written. Where once there existed a relatively comfortable arrangement of some sexual and emotional security, now the survivor is thrown unwillingly into the incredibly disruptive and time-consuming maelstrom of dating, sexual gaming, and social insecurity at a time when defenses and self image are at their lowest ebb. Anger at this unchosen situation is often made worse by sexual or intimate encounters as one is again reminded both of what is desired and what is missing.

5. Sex as a substitute for closeness   Frequently sex is seen as the requirement (price paid) for what is *really* wanted: closeness and intimacy. Many people report simply wanting literally just to "sleep with somebody."

As one person described it: "The bed is empty. There is no one to throw a leg over, snuggle in with, bump butts with in the middle of the night, hear breathing beside you, kiss on the forehead when you come back from the 3 a.m. bathroom call, and hug when the mutually dreaded alarm goes off."

All the little signs of warmth, acceptance, and sharing are gone, and their absence is shattering. It is often the search for these things that leads one to sex, rather than the reverse, and sex becomes the ticket to getting them. In fact, sex is sometimes "endured" to get to the closeness of sleeping in someone's arms.

In an attempt to recapture the sense of well being, security, or comfort, the survivor frequently repeats (almost ritualistically) the sexual behavior patterns shared with the former lover. But instead of recapturing the desired feelings of intimacy, the result is a sense of vacuousness, an incredible emptiness made even more severe by current sexual interactions that are leading nowhere.

Unfortunately, sex, usually narrowly defined as intercourse, is the only expression of intimacy and closeness many people know how to show or to receive; it is indeed the nearest thing to nurturing they have experienced. Thus they give and receive it, wondering why they still feel empty when the morning finds them staring at the ceiling wondering what they are doing there.

6. Sex as fear   Strange as it may sound, sex is often found to be an expression of fear. Getting lost in sex with someone is a powerfully distracting way to relieve one's fear of the present and future. Fear of commitment is the most common experience reported by those whose lovers have died. Having felt badly hurt by the loss of the relationship and the investment in the person, the survivor is at best skeptical and at worst terrified to begin another commitment of any depth. Even partners with whom one develops a fairly exclusive sexual understanding are constantly evaluated as to their involvement and their potential for leaving or being left.

It is as though the survivor, having lost the lover of choice, always reserves or holds back a part that will never be that committed again. The pain is experienced as too great ever to risk another loss of that kind; the hurt is too deep ever again to be that vulnerable; the loss too overwhelming to be recovered and lost again. Sex as fear is here expressed in physical interaction with no concomitant emotional involvement.

Once a new sexual relationship has begun, another fear may involve the lack of parameters on the relationship. The survivor immediately wants to set the limits, make clear the recreational nature of the sex, deny the involvement (whether real or imagined), assure himself or herself of the freedom to leave at any moment without question, or get a commitment of non-commitment from the new partner. Boundaries are quickly established either by much talking, or none at all.

The underlying dynamic in this expression of sex as a component of fear is the apprehension that the new lover will die and leave as the former one did. Some people report that, in the midst of a new relationship, they will suddenly back off and retreat for no apparent reason. Upon reflection they come to understand that the motivation for their withdrawal has to do with the frightening realization that, sooner or later, the new lover will also die or leave. Rather than face yet another loss, they choose to disengage emotionally, often maintaining some semblance of a sexual involvement that soon ends. At least, when the *survivor* breaks off the relationship, she or he feels a sense of control that is not present when the new partner leaves or dies.

Sex as fear is seen in those persons who practice serial monogamy, never quite allowing themselves to get close enough to commit, enjoying the sexual interactions, knowing all along those interactions will be ended before they are permitted to grow into involvement.

7. *Sex as nurturing* When one reaches this experience of post-death sexuality, real clarity and health are just around the corner. One may see attempts at nurturing in relationships early on, but it is usually not until the previous six tasks have been completed (in no particular sequence) that this component of sexuality is allowed to be risked.

In the months following the death of the lover, survivors consistently report a sometimes desperate sense of wanting to be nurtured; they seek sex and intimacy, carefully or indiscriminately, as a means to that end. It is only as they begin to feel more secure and able to offer themselves as valuable and worthwhile that they begin to seek out others to both *give* and receive sex as a form of nurturing.

Sex as play is a part of this nurturing. It is a sign that the survivor has begun to let go of the old self and to begin rebuilding a new identity, incorporating the death of the former lover into current life experience. The playfulness of sex only begins to occur when the survivor decides to go on with life and to risk involvement to that end. This may occur periodically throughout the early days after the death, but is only most evident after several new partners have helped the survivor move through the earlier reactions to the death.

As a new identity begins to develop without the former partner, the survivor's sexual experience is described less often as "having sex" and more frequently as "making love" with the new partner. It is at this point that the survivor may begin purposefully to seek out a new, longer term (even permanent) relationship.

Sex as giving and receiving nurturing is an important signpost for the one who has had a lover die; it is an indication that some significant bridges have been crossed and that it is time to renew a commitment to further and deeper relating.

We have here examined some of the initial reactions to the death of a lover. We will, in the next chapter, look at some guidelines for survivors to follow as they actively pursue sex after death.

11

Guidelines for Sex After Death

People handle death the same way they handle any other difficulty in their lives. If the person is an aggressive problem solver, he or she will take on grief (and sexual, intimate relationships as a part of that grief) in the same way. A person who passively reacts to other life events will more passively respond to the death of a lover, hoping that some resolution eventually will present itself.

Of course, there are variations on these two extremes. The point is that we are consistent in our handling of life's circumstances and will follow our own style of grieving as well as our own pattern of involvement with new sexual partners.

Thus the following guidelines are meant to be general suggestions that may be fitted to each person's particular style of coping. Like the ideas in the previous chapter, they have been gleaned from interactions with many survivors who have been and are still working through the death of a lover and have found the ideas to be helpful. (Also, as in the previous section, "lover" may be read "friend," "love," "partner," or "spouse"; and "sex" may be read "intimacy.")

As with any realistic discussion of sexual intimacy, it is important to assume as a basic premise that precautions will be taken against sexually transmitted disease. We know now that each time we have intercourse we are exposed to the infectious disease profile of every other person with whom our partner has had intercourse—ever—and we are likewise exposing our partner. Owing to the AIDS epidemic especially, most people who read even the most popular literature are familiar with how to prevent infection. If there is any doubt or question, printed information is readily available from physicians, pharmacists, clergy, and other professionals, and various public health or reproductive services clinics listed in the telephone directory. All of the information in this chapter is to be read in the context of taking seriously the prevention of sexually transmitted and other infectious diseases.

1. *"Give sorrow words."* Shakespeare's Macbeth says: "Give sorrow words; the grief that does not speak whispers the o'erfraught heart and bids it break." It is important to talk about the loss, talk about the feelings, the hurt, the anger, the disappointment, the sadness, the relief from the pain of a long and agonizing illness or a short, traumatic one. Survivors need to find someone to talk with who will not give advice or tell them not to feel that way.

They also need to talk with the new sexual partner, especially when experiencing any of the mechanical or emotional difficulties noted in Chapter 10. Survivors need to tell the partner about these difficulties, not to seek sympathy, but to be honest in asking for understanding. If the partner does not or will not understand, that will indicate something about the choice of partners.

To put thoughts into words, and to do self appraisal, survivors often keep a journal or buy a small notebook to jot down feelings about everything, especially intimacy and sex, every few days or so. Such a journal can be a way to keep track of dream life as well as other events that are important to remember such as dating, new sex partners, and time alone. Looking back over a few months (years, eventually) it will be helpful to see progress and change, as well as which ideas and behaviors have remained the same.

It is possible that short term counseling may be in order if problems persist, or if some objective insight is needed into thoughts, actions, and feelings. There are many excellent counselors listed in the Yellow Pages of the phone book, but it is hard to tell the duds from the pros just by their ads. Rather, encourage the survivor to ask someone who has been through a similar experience for a recommendation, or call a hospital chaplain or someone in a Hospice setting for a referral. Make it clear to the therapist that short-term counseling is the goal. A good counselor will accept stated boundaries and offer appropriate help, while at the same time gently urging the survivor to look beyond current difficulties to old life patterns that may be informing the choice of new sex partners.

Above all, it is important to talk. Grief, especially the deep grief experienced around the loss of a lover and the sexual ramifications of it, is like gas on the stomach that needs to be relieved—there's more room on the outside than there is inside. The more survivors talk, the more likely it is that their sex life after a lover's death will be satisfying.

2. _Slow down._ Often when a lover dies, survivors feel pressure (both internal and external) to hurry up and get their lives back to "normal" again. They will need help from friends to ignore the pressure and slow down. The meter is not ticking; there is no time limit or required deadline to obey.

Internally, the death leaves one empty and disoriented, missing the stability or at least relative predictability of life with the other. Of course, there is internal pressure (even panic) to recapture that lifestyle, and that is part of the search and replacement syndrome mentioned earlier. But it is important to allow space to heal and, perhaps even more importantly, time to establish a new (or at least separate) identity apart from the dead lover.

External pressure comes from supposedly well-meaning friends who want the survivor to please hurry and get re-coupled so _they_ (the friends)wwill feel better. If possible, these people are to be summarily ignored. They will only increase the sense of panic and provide occasions for further depression and anger. Real friends will understand and support survivors in their journey to renegotiate who they are sexually and otherwise at their own speed. Friends will help to acknowledge the panic, face it head on, and, in doing so, ease the pressure to re-couple.

As a part of slowing down, reevaluating the future, and examining life as a sexual being, survivors need to keep in mind that grief is intensely physical. Remembering to eat, exercise, and rest are as important to recovering libido as they are to overcoming the depression and lethargy that keep one from enjoying (or even wanting) sexual interactions.

Finally, when feeling pressured to get a date or to find a table for one in a restaurant, survivors need to be reminded that *alone* and *lonely* are not synonymous. Contrary to the image presented in telephone and diamond commercials, it is possible to spend time, even enjoyable time, alone. Time alone without sex is called celibacy, and many people are choosing it over the risk of disease or too hasty involvement. For some people, celibacy is a serious decision for a permanent lifestyle. Others alternate between periods of celibacy and periods of sexual involvement. Survivors will follow whatever variation on that theme fits. They need to be supported, however, in the belief that, regardless of internal or external pressure for sex, it is as acceptable to say "no" as it is to say "yes."

3. *Date friends first.* A major difficulty following the death of a lover is where and how to meet safe, single persons. One way to gently ease back into the social scene is to date people known a long time as friends. Good, close friends will provide nurturing and companionship without demanding sex as the price to pay for it. They are also frequently the source of other "referrals" for dating.

Survivors need to beware of most singles groups and meat market bars or parties. Both can be gathering places for personswwho are desperate for relationships. As they search for closeness, some people may be willing to go through the gaming and the disease risk of recreational sex with someone they know little about. Though most people report that such experiences lead to feeling even emptier, such activity appears to take the edge off the loneliness for a while.

Where business is involved, it is usually considered wise for survivors not to date employees or subordinates. The relationship is immediately changed, making supervision and evaluations awkward at best. Some people even recommend not dating coworkers, though this may unnecessarily restrict the number of social opportunities. In any case, it is recommended that coworkers or subordinates be approached with extreme caution for anything but casual dating. They are almost always poor choices for sexual or intimate partners.

Probably the best way for survivors to meet people is by slowly continuing to follow their own interests and interacting with the people naturally found there. If they take a course in the local community school, play golf once a week, work out at the fitness club, socialize at church, travel, attend a special interest group, or work for a candidate, they are likely to come into contact with persons who have similar interests and compatibilities.

As survivors work through the tasks described in Chapter 8, their social interactions will change somewhat. They will be attracted to different kinds of persons to provide different things at different times. However those interactions progress, the place to start is with friends.

4. *Just because someone is dead doesn't make them right.* In the course of grieving the death of a lover, people frequently believe they are in some manner still obligated to do things or maintain activities and behaviors consistent with what the lover "would have wanted me to do." While in some instances this can simply be a way of reaffirming a decision, it can also be a method of coercing oneself into doing something against one's better judgment, and resenting it later.

Just because the lover died doesn't mean that *his or her* wishes are always and forever to be followed for the rest of *the survivor's* life, especially since the survivor probably did not always do what the person wanted when the lover was alive. Survivors need to know it is all right to continue to disagree and to follow the course of best self interest, regardless of what the lover "would have wanted."

This is especially true in new sexual interactions. It may be fairly clear, for instance, that the lover would not have wanted the survivor to see other people, much less to have sex with them. Whether this expectation is meant for the short or long term, if survivors feel obligated to "respect those wishes" they will feel guilty and eventually angry at themselves, the dead lover, and the new partner.

It is important to remember that obligations to the former lover ended at death. Of course the dead lover will be respected and remembered for the rest of the survivor's life; but to arrange the new life in accordance with the dead person's wishes is to die with them and maintain an existence as a shrine to the memory of the loved one. It is vital to keep in mind that death does not confer posthumous infallibility on anyone, particularly regarding sexual activities, where the survivor's vulnerability and intimacy are potentially at greatest risk.

5. *Be honest.* No matter how difficult it is at first, survivors must be encouraged to tell the truth, to say what they want and don't want, when they want or don't want it. They need to make it clear with a new partner that the goal of the relationship is nurturing, physical contact, or companionship without the pressure of sex (at least for the present). Or they can talk about wanting the enjoyment of physically being together without commitment. If commitment is desired, they need to say so directly and check out the other person's wants and needs as openly as both persons are able.

There will be times, as noted earlier, when survivors will have flashbacks (sexual and otherwise). If these are overwhelming and cause for withdrawing for a while, partners must be told what is occurring. Likewise with feelings of fear, anger, joy, and playfulness. It is always better to know than to guess.

A commonly held guideline is: Talk rather than assume. If survivors don't say what they want, both in terms of sex and the entire relationship, they are likely to end up frustrated and disappointed. Though difficult, it is important to talk about the limits of the relationship, going out with other people, sex with others, how to handle issues of disease and birth control. The more people talk, the less anxious they will feel and the more certain they are about what is and is not going on in sexual interactions.

Finally, it is important to remember to temper honesty with a sense of humor. Many relationships die from "terminal seriosity." Survivors can learn to appreciate their imperfection and the awkwardness of the situation. It is okay not to be perfect; in fact, it's the imperfection that makes us interesting. Survivors need to be able to laugh at their own groping, and be prepared to forgive themselves and their partners when the inevitable mistakes are made.

6. *Be open.* Rather than repeating choices regarding sexual partners, types of personalities, or dating behaviors, it is important to be open to new relationships. This openness usually comes only after the searching, distraction and anger tasks have been worked through. It may only develop after short term counseling with

someone who can point up the repetition in the survivor's behavior, thereby allowing them to choose new ways of relating.

Openness to new sexual behavior happens as one becomes more playful with a new partner, having let go of some of the attachment to the past. Such behavior may include an increase or decrease in sexual activity or even different sexual activities than one has practiced before.

The attitude of openness means also broadening the definition of sex beyond that of intercourse only. Sex can mean varying types of physical interaction, with varying degrees of eroticism or with none at all. One who is grieving the death of a lover quickly learns what people with chronic diseases such as arthritis, diabetes, cancer, or heart disease have had to learn: Sex is possible in many different positions, at different tempos, and with different levels of intensity. Sexual intimacy means whatever the couple decides it means, from cuddling to intercourse to massage to sleep.

Finally, survivors need to be encouraged to be open to love resurfacing from within. Although they feel as if that ability has been permanently damaged, the truth is it is only temporarily out of order. It will surface periodically, as if coming up for air, and then only very cautiously for fear of being damaged once again. Hurt, pain, anger, and fear all serve to protect that love from too quickly rushing to the surface in its need for expression and encouragement. Survivors need to allow these feelings enough time to interact with the love, then gradually allow it to come forth.

As has been said before, it is simply not true that "time heals all wounds." What people *do* with that time will determine whether and how much healing occurs. Grieving does not automatically mean growing. The above guidelines are meant to provide some suggestions for dealing with the time in such a way as to expand the possibilities for growth and change.

Part of the survivor's grieving time is certain to be spent in intimate, sexual activity. The sex may be perceived and felt as anger, distraction, nurturing, recreation or as a part of an overall relationship with a new partner. It may be depressing at some times and invigorating at others.

There is indeed sex after death. It is important to allow that sex to be an active and supportive part of the healing process.

12

Church After Death

The dominant feeling survivors have after the death of a loved one is *vulnerability*. They may be physically weak from fatigue or lack of regular meals; they are emotionally "weak," subject to various mood changes, and unable to control or even express the different feelings that spew to the surface from deep inside their gut. Social occasions are frequently avoided and obligations postponed for fear of losing control, being "blindsided," and feeling humiliated and embarrassed when voluminous tears suddenly appear and an excuse must be made for a quick exit.

A religious service, for many persons, is not simply a social occasion or an obligation; it is a source of comfort where the chaotic world is put back in order, where familiar readings and well-worn trappings are reminders of the past and of the transcendence of God and the abiding nature of the church community they belong to.

Ideally, in this community people who knew you before the death will uphold, comfort, console, and treat you like a normal person after the death. When all other social obligations are avoided, survivors may well venture back to the church community, seeking solace and understanding when they have been unable to find it in the world around them.

What they often find in reality, however, is surprise at their own difficult reactions to the service, and a community unprepared liturgically and personally to deal with their grief. Having come expecting to find solace, survivors are astonished to note their own feelings of *anger* at Scripture readings regarding resurrections and healings, *sadness* at stories (scriptural or otherwise) of tenderness or loss, *depression* regarding flashes of memories of the presence of the loved one in the church, *hurt* and *envy* at announcements of others going on with their lives with baptisms, confirmations, and marriages, and *indignation* when a reference is made to the justice and mercy of God. These feelings are often exacerbated by familiar, meaningful songs and music that cause the spillover of tears again and again.

Many survivors report feeling isolated in the church service, met by uncertain stares from persons who want to help but don't know how, who want to comfort but don't want to increase the pain and tears, or who are embarrassed at the undignified show of emotion during an otherwise orderly service. (Some survivors recount that it was suggested they not return to church until they could keep their emotions under control.)

Greetings and questions from otherwise caring people turn out to be hackneyed, insincere, or unrealistic due to an inability to know what to say or an unwillingness to hear the truth about the survivor's deep feelings.

- "You look great! Are you feeling better now?"
- "I'll bet things are going fine, aren't they?"
- "It's time to get back and get on with your life."
- "Don't cry! He's in a much better place now."
- "I'm sure the Lord is comforting you."
- "Time heals all wounds, dear. You'll be over this soon."

It is as though people set up their questions to receive only positive answers, and to avoid confronting the desperate fear of death and grief inside themselves. Unfortunately for many survivors, the church is no different from any other social group they have been scrupulously avoiding. So, disappointed, they stop their Sunday sojourn and remain at home, unable to face the further onslaught of their feelings and insensitivity of the community in which they thought they would find solace and healing.

So that the survivor's experience of the faith community assists rather than hinders the journey through bereavement, the following suggestions are offered:

1. Decide why you're going. Though it may not be possible to determine at first, give some thought to the reasons you are returning to church. There are many possibilities: for a first step back into social relationships in a "safe" setting; for the liturgy/service itself and for your own comfort; to see people you haven't seen in a while, and perhaps would see only at church. If you have some idea of why you go to church, you will feel less befuddled when you are confronted with concerned faces and difficult questions, and you will experience a greater sense of achievement, when you leave, for having accomplished your task.

2. Prepare your response. As you already realize, supposedly well-meaning people say thoughtless things. Also, you will run into people with whom you have varying levels of acquaintance and intimacy, and will want to be able to respond differently to different situations. Some preparation—rehearsing the probable scenarios in your head—may help to relieve some of your anxiety about not being able to handle yourself, or being surprised and lost for words.

For people you know well who ask about you, it may be appropriate to say, "It's really hard, but I'm doing okay." For others, who are asking socially, you might respond, "I'm doing the best I can. Thanks for asking." Then ask about them or change the subject. For people you really want to see: "It's very hard. Would you call me at home this afternoon? I'd really like to talk with you." Some preparation regarding responses beforehand will make those first moments of greetings a bit less awkward and less overwhelming. The important thing is to give yourself permission to say different things to different people, depending on who they are and how you feel at the time. (This means it is also all right to say you're fine even though you aren't, or to tell the truth and dissolve into tears.)

3. Return gradually. It is not required to begin by attending the most crowded and visible service. Many people have found it helpful to first go back to the church building on a weekday when no one else is around and to sit in your usual seat and get the feeling of what it is like now that the loved one is not there any more. This time of private prayer, rage, sadness, or depression may be the beginning of real spiritual comfort that simply cannot be attained if others are around.

Likewise, it may be easier to attend a weekday morning or mid-week evening service where the crowd will be smaller and perhaps more focused on a specific activity in which the survivor can less obtrusively participate. On Sunday, go to the earliest service (or a Saturday or Sunday evening service) to limit the number of people you will have to speak with.

4. *Go with a friend.* Choose someone who has been through a similar experience or who knows you well enough not to be disturbed by your tears, and who acts both as a support and a buffer when you feel overwhelmed by the plethora of emotions. It may also be possible to go with a group of friends (from a guild or particular social group with which you are comfortable) who will serve the same purpose. In any case, knowing that the person sitting beside you will be accepting and available may ease the re-entry into church considerably.

5. *Leave when you want.* Unlike jails, mental hospitals, the military, and some personal-growth seminars, you are not required to stay until dismissed. Leave whenever you feel the need: if your emotions become overwhelming, if you get "blindsided" in some way, or even if the timer inside you indicates for no apparent reason that it is time to go. Leave when you have gotten what you came for: whether that was to take a first step back into the community, to hear a specific person preach, to receive communion, to hear your granddaughter sing in the choir, to watch the Christmas pageant, or just to sing a hymn or two. Leave before or during the last hymn if you are not up to greeting people or answering questions. To do this inconspicuously, it may be a good idea to arrive a little late and sit toward the back (though in most churches you have to get there *early* to get a seat in the back).

6. *Stay regardless.* Although this may seem the opposite of number five, it is actually a corollary of it. The point is that it is all right to stay *or* go. If you need to leave, do it. But remember that you have a right to be there emoting up a storm, crying through hymns, blowing your nose during the sermon, and sitting when others are standing or kneeling just because your legs won't hold you up. It is, after all, *your* church too, and it is precisely the place where it is (or ought to be) okay to bring *all* of your emotions to be offered up to

God for blessing and healing. Decide that you need to experience and express your emotions, that it is in fact a requirement to do so if you are to survive the death of the loved one, and go ahead and feel what you are feeling—*especially* in church. The idea here is to be aware of your personal need at the time. Some days you will be more able and willing to stay and cry (especially if a friend is there beside you) and other days you will need to make a prompt exit. Either one is okay with God.

7. *Go someplace new.* Returning to the church where you used to worship may be too painful, too emotionally complicated, or simply no longer comfortable or appropriate. Contrary to common wisdom, it is not required to go back. One couple (whose child died) joined a different church where only one or two people knew of their circumstance. While the hymns and order of service were the same and thus filled with former meaning and memories, the new surroundings and new faces they encountered fitted their sense of eventually becoming new people.

The important thing is not to feel obligated or stuck, but rather to do what spiritually feels best, and to find the community in which healing can best occur. For many people, possibly depending on their network before the death, that will be to return to their former place of worship. For many others, it will mean to find a different community where they can be seen and known as the person they now are, rather than the person they—along with the loved one—used to be.

Whether you have a lifetime of memories established in a particular church setting, or "going to church" (or now a different church) is a relatively new experience for you, there will come a time when spiritual resources may be needed. Remember that "the Sabbath was made for man, not man for the Sabbath"; you may have access to those spiritual resources in whatever way is most meaningful to you and on your own time schedule; there is no right or wrong way to do it. Give yourself the freedom to experience the healing of memories and relationships—with friends, the loved one, and God—at any level at which you feel ready, regardless of how much that level may change from day to day.

I hope these guidelines will allow you to seek and find nurturing in community with others, to find the place that nurtures you, recognizing that it may be a different setting than the one that met your needs in the past. As with the other (physical, social, psychological) areas of change, it is important to allow your spiritual framing and understanding of life to grow and change in response to the indelible experience of death and the incredible journey toward survival.

13

Surviving
Death

The young woman, weak and
dying, reaches out from her hospital bed for her sobbing husband. He bends over her, wrapping his arms around her thin
frame as she cries: "I'm so sorry. I'm so sorry. I didn't mean to
leave you like this." He answers: "I know. I love you. It's
okay. I love you."

Three hours later, having lapsed into a coma, she takes her
final breath and dies. For her it is over. For her husband a new
task has just begun. The task is survival.

There are no courses in how to survive deep losses. Most of the
literature on grief and bereavement is either coldly clinical, unrealistically emotional, or piously religious. Grieving persons are
described either in terms of aberrant behavior or with such faith as
to make the rest of us appear hopeless. Cultural guidelines are
unclear or nonexistent, and advice from friends is frequently con-
tradictory.

It is possible, however, to get some clarity about the task of survival from those who are going through it. You will note that we
did not say "have gone through it." Surviving deep loss is always a
present task. One does not "get over it," "recover from it," or "go
on" in the usual decisive sense of those phrases, as if one were dealing with a broken arm, a scab that will come off, a bruise that will
go away, or even a long term illness from which gradual return to
health is possible. Once a deep loss has been sustained, the experi-

ence of it will continue to recur periodically, calling on the best coping resources the person has available.

Some of the people who are facing the task of surviving the death of a spouse, child, parent, or friend meet together monthly to share their reactions and experiences in local bereavement groups sponsored by hospitals and hospices. The following suggestions, comments and observations from those groups help shed light on a largely uncharted path, and provide relief in the affirmation that we are not alone in the sometimes bizarre feelings and behaviors that accompany the daily struggle to survive death.

1. *"Give sorrow words."* This advice from *Macbeth,* discussed in Chapter 11, relates to surviving more than just sexual encounters. It is an important (perhaps the most important) strategy for gradually coming to terms with the loss.

Whether the survivor talks to a friend, family member or professional (psychologist, pastoral counselor, psychiatrist), it would be well to choose one or two persons with whom to "check in" periodically. Meeting weekly (eventually monthly) at a regular time allows space for ventilation, support, affirmation, and feedback. The person chosen must be one who will not give advice, tell the survivor how to feel, or be upset by the frequent expression of gut wrenching tears and sorrow. An honest listener will ask questions and point out possible dangers the survivor may not see due to the emotional obfuscation of grieving.

Often it is difficult for the survivor to continue to talk after many months have passed. Feeling as though he or she should be "over it" or coping better" by now, the person may be reluctant to keep going over the same (old) themes. It is necessary to reassure the survivor at these times that the listener is not bored with the inconclusive repetition of painful events or angry that the survivor has not totally come to terms with a particular feeling or issue.

Talking with someone who will really listen, even when they don't understand or agree, is a way to relieve the stress, share the fear, and bear the loneliness. Talking and listening are gifts that enrich both givers and receivers immeasurably.

2. *Grief is physical.* Most people expect bereavement to be a time of deep emotional exhaustion, and indeed this is true. They are,

therefore, usually ready for the emotional roller coaster of highs and lows, the fragility of their feelings, and the emotional emptiness inside. What they don't expect is the constant tiredness, lethargy, and lack of initiative. The body seems to require inordinate hours of sleep (and at odd times) to physically process all the emotional turmoil. Even persons who sleep well may complain of lying in bed for long periods of time just staring into space, resting and thinking.

Grief is hard work both emotionally *and* physically. This is especially true after a lengthy illness during which time people may not have realized the stress under which they functioned. The survivor needs to allow time for rest and, if possible, to let sleep come whenever it will.

Occasionally, survivors will experience the same symptoms of the disease from which their loved one died. They may even think that they are coming down with the same thing and will soon, therefore, die themselves. Friends and supporters can tell the survivor that this occurrence is not unusual, but it is also important to recommend seeing a physician for complete verification. It is helpful, in addition, to allow the survivor to talk about the symptoms and their meaning in relationship to the dead loved one (identification, the wish to be dead and be with him or her).

If what comes *out* of the survivor's mouth (talk) is the most important strategy for the tasks of grieving, then what goes *into* it runs a close second. A major problem most survivors report regarding food is remembering to eat. Initially following the death, of course, the person often feels too upset or weary to ingest any but small portions at odd intervals. A cultural understanding of this fact is shown by the way friends bring food to the mourner's house, often to be frozen for later. During this time friends may encourage (not insist) and remind the survivor to eat, and, as a way to facilitate that, eat *with* the survivor.

As days and weeks pass, the reason for not eating changes from lack of interest to the dislike of cooking for one. Underlying the reality of going to the trouble of meal preparation for one person is the symbolic nature of food and its association with the loved one.

Food is seen as a form of nurturing. It is often a symbolic reward for accomplishments or a way of celebrating a particular event. The survivor often does not want to be nurtured, feels no desire for reward, and certainly has nothing to celebrate. Thus, in addition to avoiding single meal preparation, the survivor may also feel reluctant to go out to dinner. Likewise, the thought of sitting down at a table for one, whether out or at home, revives pleasant (now painful) associations of occasions with the loved one. It is no wonder that the survivor avoids, forgets, or refuses meals.

And yet, because grief is so physical it is important not only to maintain a healthy diet but also to exercise regularly. These two factors (diet and exercise) can reduce the stress associated with grieving and maintain a healthy enzyme, hormone, and chemical balance that will have a positive effect on both the experiencing and handling of emotions. Prudent diet and exercise routines should always be confirmed by the survivor's physician.

3. Just because someone is dead doesn't make them right. Although discussed in Chapter 11 regarding sexual behavior, this notion quite obviously has much broader connotations for the survivor. Not only related to socializing, the idea impacts the investment of money, work and living arrangements, purchase of clothes or other items, and travel and leisure plans. Again, the fact that your loved one died does not mean that *his or her* wishes need be followed the rest of *your* life.

Many people conjure up this aphorism as a means of providing some safe boundaries for their behavior immediately following the death. Frequently, survivors fear they will behave foolishly without the counterbalance of the former loved one. They keep old rules and guidelines intact by constantly asking what the dead person would have wanted them to do.

The fact is that seldom do survivors use the loss of boundaries that occurs with the death as an excuse for aberrant or highly unusual behavior. Most people remain consistently within their own behavioral limits regardless of outside circumstances. While in some instances the nature of the death or the relationship may result in a temporary extension beyond the usual limits, these occurrences are rare. Most people stay who they are, though they may now have the time and opportunity to expand upon parts of themselves (art, travel, spirituality, study) they never felt able or willing to explore before. It is, therefore, important that this phrase not be used to stifle this exploration.

Usually, as some old boundaries are reinforced and others, by testing out new ideas or relationships, are expanded, the real or imagined wishes of the dead person become less and less of an issue in decision making.

Many survivors use the "one year rule" as an initial guideline, based on the experience of those who have preceded them in the grieving process. This rule suggests making *no major decisions for one year* following a significant loss or death. Because that first year is so incredibly emotional, physically draining, and a time when identity and psychological balance are being reexamined and reevaluated, the survivor is thought to need the protection of the full year's time and space before major decisions are considered. As one person said: "I was so emotionally unstable and mentally disconnected that year I could barely decide what clothes to wear to work. I can see that now, but I couldn't then. I'm glad I knew to wait."

Of course some major decisions may not be able to be delayed. Good friends who either are or know competent attorneys, financial planners, and counselors may need to be consulted and trusted to help. Usually, however, decisions about moving, investments, whether and where to work, and especially romantic relationships, can be postponed until one year has elapsed and some of the turmoil and confusion have cleared.

4. It is possible to feel opposite emotions simultaneously. Unfortunately most people in this culture have been taught to believe that their feelings exist in an either-or dichotomy. Thus if they feel extreme sadness about the death, they wonder how they can feel extreme relief at the same time. If they feel love for the person who has died, how can they also feel anger? The fact is that people do feel both sadness and relief, love and anger, hope and despair all at once as they react and respond to the different parts of themselves working to make sense out of what has happened.

As they yo-yo from elation to depression and back again their emotions are usually right on the surface, sensitive and volatile. Sometimes it feels good to feel bad and often it feels bad to feel good. It is important that the survivor have permission and support to feel many things at once. It is then useful to take the time to sort those feelings out by talking with someone or through some creative expression such as keeping a journal, drawing or painting the feelings, or working them out in clay.

5. *Releasing pain is not erasing memory.* Strange as it may sound, most people are apprehensive about giving up intense grieving. They believe that their grief, however publicly or privately portrayed, is a sign of their caring for the dead loved one. To give it up or even lessen it might be seen by themselves and others as diminishing that caring. Likewise there is the fear that to release the pain will mean relinquishing the person's memory.

The physical pain of grieving, especially crying, may indeed be the only sense of sustained contact the survivor still feels with the person who died. To experience sadness, tears, depression, emptiness, and despair is to maintain a powerful connection of presence with the loved one. It is feared that to lessen the pain is to diminish that connection and lose contact forever. To the survivor of a deep loss, the pain and depression are far preferable to the anticipated sense of increased emptiness that might come with a decision to let go of these feelings.

In fact the exact opposite is true. Releasing pain gradually allows time and space for more pleasant and vivid memories to surface. The loved one's memory becomes more a realistic part of daily living and less a chore to be remembered. The sense of continued contact with and caring about the memory of the loved one also becomes more realistic and there is less panic about feeling bad in order to "safeguard" the relationship, lest it somehow slip away.

A commonly related experience of survivors seems to occur at the three-year mark following the death of the loved one. (It may occur earlier or later, depending on the particular style of grieving of the individual.) Moving into the fourth year, survivors report that they are doing quite well, feeling better, adjusting, handling the day-to-day affairs of life with some good ability now, perhaps even getting into a meaningful, long-term relationship with someone, and then suddenly find themselves deep in the midst of another devastating depression.

They think they are going crazy, that they have had a severe relapse, or have somehow been psychologically tricked into thinking they were recovering when, obviously, they are back to square one again after all this time. Friends and supporters need to assure the survivor that *none* of these things is true. What they are experiencing is *grieving the loss of the grieving*.

It is as though the grief has become, if not a friend, at least a known, familiar companion on the journey for this long period of time. The feelings, behaviors, depressions, and difficult times of the year have become known, anticipated, and expected. To begin moving beyond those feelings, to begin letting them go, replacing them with new ways of relating and feeling, is to experience the loss of that "companion" which has been intimately present on a daily basis for the three years. And that involves some grieving for this, another, loss.

6. *It's okay to feel suicidal.* Just because survivors *feel* suicidal doesn't mean they *are* suicidal. Feelings are *not* facts. To want to die is a normal response to deep loss. Along with maintaining painful feelings, death seems the only certain way to be back with the loved one again.

Often the desire to die, as paradoxical as it sounds, is also a statement of strength. It can be a sign of wanting to regain control over a life that has felt uncontrollable. A common phrase used to describe suicide is: "He took his life into his own hands." When contemplating dying, that is exactly what the survivor is expressing. Thus, rather than quickly admonishing the survivor for talking about suicide, friends need to listen openly to this expression of desire for an end to grief and encourage the person to talk openly about it. Care should be taken, of course, to insure that the survivor does not *act* on such an impulse. Frequently, simply sharing the desire diminishes the possibility of seriously carrying it out. In any case, referral to a competent professional counselor must be offered and encouraged.

For the same reason it is okay to "wallow." Having sustained a deep loss, it is perfectly normal to feel despairing, depressed, and incredibly sad. Instead of denying or discounting the feelings, it is important to let them surface a while, and to spend some time talking about them with someone who understands that the person is not crazy, just grieving. A good wallow will help the survivor feel better later.

7. *Time doesn't heal—it merely passes.* As has been mentioned before in discussing recovery from death, the old truism that "time heals all wounds" is untrue. In fact, at least for the first year or two, time makes it worse. The passage of days and weeks filled with anniversaries, holidays, special remembrances, and things that were planned to have been done together only makes the death more vivid and the loss more real.

There are certain variables that can provide guidelines for anticipating, very generally, the kind of grieving experience the survivor may have. Such things as the length of the relationship, the depth and intensity of the relationship, the cause and type of death, and the length of the period of dying will all interact with the problem-solving style of the individual to produce different grieving experiences in different people.

The most important variable, however, is that of communication. How well did the dying person communicate with the survivor in their normal lives together? What did they talk about as the dying process occurred? Did they talk about what the survivor was to do without the loved one? Was there talk of going on without one another? Or were these issues avoided, due to the sadness and pain they would surely evoke?

Survivors seem to do better if there has been some clear communication, of whatever depth, during the dying, about surviving, what that may be like and what the wishes of the dying person are. Even if those wishes are highly restrictive, at least they are known and can be openly discussed with a friend or counselor.

Many people describe deep loss "as though someone cut something out of me and left a gaping, bleeding hole." Such wounds will not passively heal themselves with the mere passage of time. They need active attention and mending. Forgiveness, love, creativity, sharing, relationships: These are the threads that will suture the wound and mend it, so that healing can begin. Time will pass. How the survivor actively fills that time will determine whether and how healing occurs.

8. Expect to be "blindsided." One of the most embarrassing and frightening experiences of deep loss is to be perfectly normal one minute and, for no apparent reason, emotionally dissolved the next. It is as though a part of the survivor is always on the lookout for tender or painful remembrances. The survivor may be in a restaurant or in the car when a song comes on the radio, doing dishes or other housework alone, visiting friends, hearing the phone ring or watching t.v., when suddenly some part of the person makes a connection and the person becomes teary or sad, usually without knowing why.

Depending on the situation and the memory, the feeling can be fleeting or longer lasting. In either case, the survivor needs to allow it to run its course, preferably by telling the incident to someone. It is important to know that it is okay, that it is normal, that it will pass and that it will happen with less and less frequency.

One of the most important ways friends can help is to offer the "2 A.M. Insurance Policy." They can tell the survivor: "Here is my phone number. It is okay to call me if you're having a difficult time—even at 2 A.M. I can't change it and I can't fix it, but I can listen to you and that's even more important, regardless of the hour." This simple action has helped many survivors make it through otherwise unbearable times. Chances are they will never actually call, but it makes a great deal of difference to know that they can do so if necessary.

9. Laughing is not disrespectful. Even though someone has died, funny things will continue to happen at work, at home, to others, and even to the survivor. It is okay to laugh at these things without feeling guilty or disrespectful to the person for not spending twenty-four hours a day grieving. Humor is a great stress reducer; it is another of the active sutures necessary to help close the wound and heal. Besides, glumness is boring; but suture self.

10. Not less pain, only less frequent. As discussed in Chapter 11, there is no "normal" time for the "completion" of grieving. Different people with different kinds of losses and relationships will grieve for different periods of time.

It is extremely important for the survivor to know and remember that, while the loss may not become any less painful, the occasions of experiencing that pain become less frequent. Especially during times of deep despair, friends may remind the survivor that he or she will feel different a year from now—not necessarily "better," but certainly different. The depth of the pain never decreases; when the person gets in touch with the loss from time to time, the depth of feeling is the same. The only change is that the times she or he gets in touch with it will be spaced further and further apart.

And there is some comfort in this fact. A part of the survivor will always remember the relationship with the loved one as it was at the time of the death. Another part moves on, not forgetting or denying the pain and grief, but rather incorporating and integrating it into the whole of life's experience.

11. Life is too short not to. This phrase is a helpful one for survivors to remember when faced with spontaneous, perhaps even fun, decisions, especially when they have the opportunity to do something they've been reluctant to do before, or when a new idea or experience is presented for their consideration. Because something doesn't fit with one's former image or would not have been done when the loved one was alive is no reason to reject it now. Gradually the survivors will find themselves actually beginning to enjoy some (not all, of course) of these people and experiences. They will also have fewer regrets regardless of how long or short their own lives turn out to be.

12. Remember, only you will remember. As days turn into months and years, survivors need not be surprised or disappointed when they are the only ones who remember the date of the loved one's birthday, the wedding anniversary, the time of the year they took that special vacation together, and the date of the death.

Special friends will still be there to talk with about these dates when they occur year after year. But the dates were important only to the survivor and the other person, and they generally will be remembered only by the survivor, just as the survivor alone will remember the silly, funny, tender, and sad things about the person who died. It is not that other people don't care; they simply don't care the way the survivor did.

As the above statements indicate, there are commonalities in responding to deep loss and there is some comfort for grieving persons in that knowledge. It is important to remember, however, that each person will experience loss in his or her own individual way, with nuances, feelings, and memories that are special to their particular situation.

14

Afterlife

When a loved one dies, questions arise in the survivor's mind that, even if they had been there before, were never pressing, relevant, or even meaningful. The questions are practical, logical, and theological, having to do with afterlife. They used to be topics of idle speculation, but now they are of central importance. Sitting across the table from an empty chair, walking down the hall past the vacant bedroom of a child, sitting alone in a theater waiting for a movie to start, driving home in an empty car to a dark house: these are the times the mind wanders—and wonders.

Often people are embarrassed by their questions, as though they should have the answers themselves already, or should have learned them in church or in the common culture, and are ashamed that they obviously weren't listening the day these issues were discussed. Sometimes survivors feel intimidated, fearful that if they asked the questions on their minds, God would punish them for their unbelief or their theological stupidity. So they wonder in agonizing silence, ashamed and afraid, yet forever unsettled by the nagging non-sequiturs called forth by trying to align their experience of loss with the Scriptures they read and the sermons they hear.

In fact, the church is equally unsettled by the issues of afterlife. If it were not uncertain (and perhaps ashamed and embarrassed), there would be much more sermonizing, discussion, and proclamation of belief about what happens after someone dies.

The purpose of this chapter is to bring these questions out in the open so that survivors will not feel stupid or alone in their thoughts, and to offer some reasonable possibilities to replace uncertainty with focused thought and concern, if not with clarity.

As survivors have discussed this in my office over the past twenty years, usually behind closed doors, their (and my) questions about afterlife seem to fall into six categories: purpose, place, time, safety, knowledge, and future.

1. *Purpose* Why did this death happen? Why did God make or let it happen? Was God trying to get my attention? Am I somehow to blame? Is God punishing me for something I did (or the dead person did) years ago? Did God know that something awful would happen to her in the future and therefore spare that agony by "taking" her now? Is this part of God's "plan" for him? For me? What is the meaning of this loss? What am I supposed to learn from this?

Most of these questions assume that God is in charge of everything and personally pulls strings (or perhaps now pushes buttons) that cause events (births, deaths, accidents, windfalls) that directly affect our personal lives for specific reasons, usually related to a "plan." If that is true, then God is not only capricious but also vindictive: the Divine Parent constantly chastising and recording mistakes for future retributive paybacks.

It makes more theological sense to say that "Life is unfair" and "God chooses powerlessness." People are not "rewarded" for good behavior with protection from illness, accident, misfortune, and death. In fact, that is not God's promise, as Jeremiah and others were slow to learn. Because there are things far worse than death from which we need protection, God promises instead to "be with us" *through* all of these events, in the very midst of what we experience as the unfairness of life, and as we "walk through the valley of the shadow of death." God's power is found in *presence*, not in prevention or punishment, but in choosing to be powerless and to trust us with freedom rather than devising a scheme of marionette-like manipulation as the way to be with us.

The *reason* for the death is to be found in the incident itself: physical or emotional illness, accident, carelessness. The disease took over, the mechanism malfunctioned, her attention was elsewhere, he was being mugged, she hated herself. Seldom is the reason related to, or the fault of, the survivor. When it is, the church offers confession, forgiveness, absolution, reconciliation—and always God's presence. *Never* is the reason to teach us a lesson, or to provide a situation of suffering, disability, or death for the specific edification and spiritual growth of another person. To assume this is not only to assume a God of meanness and cruelty, it is also to show incredible narcissism and religious self-righteousness disguised as piety on the part of the person who is not sick or afflicted.

The *meaning* of the loss is to be found in our reaction to it. The death itself has *no purpose*, but it may have great impact on and meaning for the lives of others, reminding us of the fragile nature of our existence, of the futility of hatred or violence, of the indomitability of the human spirit, and of the eternal nature of healing love, a part of which is found in a continuing relationship of trust with the God from whom "nothing can separate us."

2. *Place* For most people, common questions are: Where is she? Did my loved one go to a "place"? Do dead persons exist in a suspended state? Do they look like the "spirit beings" portrayed in such movies as *Cocoon* or *Close Encounters* or *The Abyss*? What does the essence of the person consist of? When exactly does it "leave" the body? Does a part of it stay here? What do people "do" in whatever "place" they are? Do they continue to "grow," to mature as time passes? Is there any such thing as "time" in that "place"? Do babies who die grow up and become adults? What about fetuses?

Attempts to answer these questions have taken different forms (usually resulting in dogmas) at different historical moments. Although my own views are presented here, it is important first to state some generalities.

First, beware of anyone claiming to have the absolute truth about any of this. There are no "right" answers, only reasoned speculation based on belief, creed, or Scripture of one brand or another. Second, take nothing literally. The importance of speculation about afterlife and its specifics is in its metaphorical impact, and the effect that speculation has on how we live our lives now. Metaphor is always more powerful than rigid literalism, and nowhere is this more evident than in the rich scriptural metaphorical images of afterlife. Third, remember that, whatever the concept we may have of that "place," it is probably not anywhere near the reality we will face when we get there, so figure in a high "humility factor" in all of this discussion. Having said that, let us venture forth, basing our images on hundreds of conversations with dying persons and the questions posed by their families after the death of the patient.

Assuming that the soul (or spirit) of the loved one is some kind of essence (though not necessarily matter), it has to *be* someplace. But the nature of that place (not to mention the nature of the essence) is, at least to me, specifically unknown. It does seem that the place must either be "in God's presence" or "outside God's presence"; either in light or darkness, what others may describe as heaven or hell.

If the "place" is in God's presence, then the essence/spirit must exist in perpetual light, surrounded by what has already been described in the best metaphorical manner possible (in various religious Scriptures from the Bible to the Hindu Baghavad Gita) as wonderful music, indescribable joy, full contentment, beatific peace, angelic safety, and eternal worship of God. It would also seem that they may know God more fully than we do now, not because they are "closer" (no one can get closer to God; we are all equidistant), but because the plane of their understanding and experience may be unhindered by the distractions of this life.

If the "place" is outside of God's presence, the essence/spirit must be in eternal darkness; not hellfire and brimstone, but eternal numbness with no interaction, much like being totally insensate, unable to touch or know anyone or anything (including one's own self), wandering in infinite shadow without impediment or obstacle, never able to know or find the light, yet always knowing it is there.

It seems to me that where the person goes is always a choice. We choose light or darkness with each business, personal, professional, or familial decision we make every day. Even at our death, it is easy to imagine that we are yet again offered an alternative. Perhaps even in the midst of eternal darkness the voice of God calls to us—the only sound able to penetrate—so that even then we may choose to ignore the sound, continuing to prefer the all-enveloping anonymity of nothingness.

People who have had children die often ask if their child will "grow up" in heaven. A man whose 16-week-pregnant wife died in a car wreck wanted to know what happened to her and the fetus? I expressed my belief that the fetus, having not been born, and not yet a person or an entity, went nowhere. (Other people may believe that the fetus is "ensouled" from conception, in which case the "soul" would go into the place of light as described above.) It would not grow and develop. Just as the body tissues of adults die, so did the fetal tissue.

But what of his wife? Would her spirit continue to age so that, assuming they were reunited at his death, they would be the same age?

These questions grow out of our need to make logical sense out of things that are beyond our logic, to temporalize the eternal, anthropomorphize the spiritual, measure death in terms of life as we experience it. While, of course, there are no certain answers, it seems to me that our spirit is eternal and ageless, so that, while our bodies age and grow, our spirits, when they meet, are the same "age," whether the body stopped at three days or ninety years.

It also makes sense that spirits continue to "grow" in their knowledge of God. If God is infinite wisdom, and our souls are "with God" (whether embodied or not), then it seems that the journey of the soul is one toward greater knowledge, feeling, and understanding of God, which, by definition, takes an eternity.

Other people will suggest that the spirit immediately obtains infinite knowledge upon its release from the body. But this is to discount and denigrate bodily existence, to continue the Greek mind/body distinction, and pronounce the life of the spirit superior. In fact, the spirit and the body are one when alive and interacting with others here. Perhaps the body is even a necessity in the body/soul journey, experiencing and learning things about God that cannot be learned in any other way, no matter how long that body journey lasts. When the body dies, the soul/essence/spirit continues the journey; and it continues in eternal light/heaven/in God's presence, unless it has chosen eternal darkness. Even there, the journey (God's search for us) continues.

3. *Time* The issue of place often raises the question of time.

When does the soul/spirit start, begin its journey? Does it exist before conception? At conception? After birth? It is easy to dismiss these questions by saying that they make no sense from an eternal perspective, that they are unanswerable in our limited understanding of things, and that they ultimately make no difference anyway—we will find out when we get there. But they are troubling for persons who have suffered the death of a loved one, and therefore bear addressing, if not answering.

I would suggest that souls are eternal, beginning and ending in God, and that we cannot say or know *when* we have a soul any more than we can know when a fetus becomes a baby, or when we fall in love with someone. Speculations and arguments on these issues have filled greater pages than these, and will continue to do so. But it is important to say that bodies and souls are of one piece, that neither precedes or is superior to the other. It may be that the two develop together, or that the energy (matter, essence) for body and soul are of the same piece and source, differentiating as our other parts do during gestation and separating at death. The eternal matter of the body continues into other matter on earth, and the eternal matter of the spirit continues into other matter in light or darkness.

Two questions regarding place have to do with activity and well-being. Survivors frequently ask, "What does he *do* there?" and "Is she safe?" "Is he okay?"

4. *Safety*   I assume that, whether in light or darkness, the spirit/essence is under God's purview and therefore "safe." (Again, Paul's words: "Nothing can separate us....") There is no such thing as eternal torment, or sadness, or missing, or grief; those things are reserved for this earthly plane of our existence. Once death has occurred, the spirit has a different perspective on that previous plane of life, a broader one limited now only by the infinity of God. Metaphorical images for that perspective are found in such words as peace, joy, rest, happiness, tranquility, and do not so much indicate inactivity as lack of worry or stress or interruption or demand.

Activity as well can only be described in metaphor. Many people imagine "heaven" as sort of a parallel universe to this one, where activities go on much the same as they do here. The jokes we have devised describe our belief in this image. But it seems that a spirit would spend eternity "being" rather than "doing." Perhaps "being" in the presence of God, regardless of whether we are here now or in eternal light (or even in darkness) is the ultimate activity we can know. So the answer to what souls *do* is that they *be*.

5. *Knowledge* Questions abound regarding the connections between "here" and "there." Can my loved one contact me? Does he know what I'm doing now? Does she know what I'm thinking and feeling? Does he "watch after" the children and me? Can they "intervene" or protect us?

In one sense, there is no difference between "here" and "there." We are not and cannot be "closer to God," or any more "with God," or nearer "home" than we are now. But in another sense, that plane of existence is broader, more inclusive, and of such a different perspective as to make contact or communication with this one pointless. But that is not to say that we are not still connected in some way (that is a mystery to be lived rather than a problem to be explained). Indeed there is always an interconnectedness of the living and the dead so that praying, caring, rejoicing, remembering, and loving are still the common ground—the shared activity—of the "communion of saints."

We do continue our lives here in the midst of a "cloud of witnesses," but there seems to be no real need for contact from that arena of existence. To do so would indelibly affect the course of the person's life here, much as a "miraculous intervention" from God would do, and would seem to violate the freedom of choice with which both we and the universe are created and endowed.

Many people want there to be continued interaction to finish unfinished business, work out emotional and personal issues with the dead loved one, or continue to converse through the healing period of bereavement. As part of the continuing nature of our connectedness it is important to do all of these things, but also it is important to assume that the dead person now has a different perspective, a more inclusive understanding of the relationship, and that they wish for us benevolence, wish for us the understanding that they now have, wish for us the equanimity, forgiveness, peace, and healing that they now know—even in the midst of their knowing our grief for them. Indeed, if there is any "grieving," it is a description of their desire that we could experience as they do now.

It seems to me that the spirit would "know" what we are doing and how we feel in a similar sense that God "knows" those things, but not in the intensely personal and perhaps judgmental way that we know and interact now. It is "knowing" in the sense of understanding, accepting without comment or response, and having such a broad view of existence that a response is neither required nor desirable.

The same is true for intervention and protection. We see and judge the events of our lives in categories of good/bad, wrong/right, fortunate/unfortunate, undeserved/deserved. We try to ward off "bad" things happening through many means: worry, data collection to avoid failures, vigilance, alertness, health habits, and prayer. Another means of warding off untoward happenings is through the hope that our loved ones can intervene and protect us from what we view from our perspective as "bad" events. But with the loved one now experiencing the perspective of eternity, neither intervention or protection are necessary, even if they were possible.

6. Future The final series of questions about afterlife have to do with the future. Will I see him again? Is he now with the rest of the family? Will all the generations of our family be together? Are suicides treated differently? Will I see her if she took her own life? What about resurrection? What about reincarnation?

Again, we define the unknown in terms with which we are familiar. But rather than "seeing" the persons again, perhaps we are "with" them; perhaps we "know" them, "experience" them in a manner that is even clearer than seeing. I doubt that we will recognize the person by face or clothing or voice, but it does seem clear that, because each spirit/essence is unique, we will "know" the person in totality, even as we will be known and experienced by others. (Paul again: "Now we see through a mirror dimly, then we will see face to face....")

Relationships, however, are for the plane of existence on which we now live. They are a way of defining who we are, designating territoriality, and setting societal limits to behavior. Once again, from the perspective of eternity (whether in light or darkness), these relationships have no usefulness or practical purpose. Where we are all one in relationship to God, previous familial and societal designations are meaningless. Recognition of specific spirit/ essences will be known, but not with the designation of relationships. The Rev. William Bausch suggests that these new kinds of relationships, "even from a startling, unimagined point of view, will be valid and true and perhaps made more intense in the context of a wildly new perspective of the connectedness of us all in God."

The manner of one's death is irrelevant. One can argue that we all participate in our own demise. If you have ever drunk alcohol, used drugs of any kind (including caffeine), smoked a cigarette, driven or ridden in a vehicle powered by an internal combustion or jet engine, eaten processed foods, or avoided exercise, then you have hastened your death. Active suicide, particularly in the case of terminal or incurable illness, is different only in its immediacy, and cannot warrant eternal condemnation in darkness any more than smoking or refusing to wear helmets, seat belts, or condoms.

Thus it seems that persons who die by suicide, or by active or passive euthanasia, or by refusing medical treatment for fatal illnesses, or by accident due to their own fault or the fault of others, or by following deleterious health habits, will be there for us, and with us. The eternal dimensions of forgiveness and understanding by far outdistance our pious judgementalness and shortsighted sense of justice.

Reincarnation does not make sense in this system, but that is because I live in a culture that generally does not believe in karmic laws. I would suggest that the spirit's journey conjoined as one with the body is necessary toward understanding God, but that the length of time or amount of accomplishment is irrelevant. One need not "return" to another body to complete a period of time to learn what is necessary, or to accomplish tasks necessary to complete the earthly understanding of God. From the perspective of eternity, perhaps one second of birth is equal to a lifetime, as one molecule of water is equal to the experience of the whole ocean. If this is the case, then reincarnation is unnecessary.

Resurrection is usually described as occurring at the "end time" when a final judgment occurs, universal equilibrium is achieved, and the living and the dead are reunited eternally in peace. There seems to be some discrepancy about whether the dead are somewhere in graves or cremation urns and then are resurrected, or are in "heaven" with God (but not quite with God), and resurrection is the final passage to being with God.

Perhaps a better image than resurrection is one of reuniting, where the embodied become spirit/essence and now have the same eternal understanding and "being" as those who have "gone before," where the distinctions of death and life have no meaning, but are included in "being" into eternity together with others and with God.

This event is usually based in the belief of a plan or purpose that must be accomplished before it occurs. Some believe it is when we finally destroy our planet and life dies out, or when the sun burns itself out and all life comes to an end here. In any case, the metaphor is the same: a reuniting of those still embodied with those who have already died. It is a hope of eternal peace and eternal connectedness, of which we may have glimpses even now. It is another symbol of the inseparable nature of God's love being stronger than death because it encompasses death, includes it, connects it ("the living with the dead"), and thereby transcends it.

Although this discussion of afterlife focuses on speculation regarding what happens after we die, it is actually about the certainty of how we live here and now. The questions we raise about our loved ones and the answers with which we address those questions are valuable and make sense only as we relate them to day-to-day living. For the truth is that we will not know what happens after we die until we die, and no amount of speculation can prepare us for that experience. What matters is what we do in the meantime, together, now. It is only in this present connected context that our wandering through the metaphors of afterlife makes sense, for now is—eternally—the only time we have.

15

The End

I could think of no more appropriate title for the final chapter of a book on death. It is hoped, however, that this ending will instead be a beginning for you; a beginning of further study, of insight and decision making regarding your own death planning, of consciousness raising in churches and community groups, of the intentional living of life until death.

But before ending, I want to briefly (and admittedly with only a surface rendering) acknowledge three other issues that need much further explication by others in the field. They are *Children, AIDS, and Long-Term Reactions.*

1. Children The focus of this book has been primarily upon the reaction of adults to death, dying, and surviving the death of a loved one. But readers will undoubtedly ask what to tell their children about death, whether or not to take them to the hospital to visit dying people, or to the funeral home to see the dead body.

Although I am not an expert on children, my experience working with them at the hospital indicates three guidelines regarding their involvement in this process:

- Ask the child what she or he believes about the event.
- When in doubt, tell the truth.
- Listen for feelings of guilt.

Children will make up their own explanation of the events surrounding the death of a loved one, and the reaction of adults to that death. Thus it is important to *ask* the child what the child thinks happened. The answer might be more accurate or at least more satisfying than your own. Feel free to confess that your best guess at an explanation is still confusing for you, thus teaching the child that there are such things as inexplicable mysteries in our universe.

Also, tell the truth. Do not say "going to sleep," "passing away," called Home," "gone to live with Jesus," or "gone to take care of other little boys and girls in heaven." These phrases, and others like them, can be very unsettling and even threatening to the child, who usually takes them literally. Instead, tell the truth about death. The sooner the child realizes death is a normal, natural part of our life together, the sooner he or she will begin to seek accurate, realistic information about it and come to terms with it.

Do not shield the child from the events, as it will usually make things seem worse, given what the child is imagining about them. Often the reason children are frightened and apprehensive about death is because they are reflecting the views and feelings of the adults around them. If adults are shielding themselves from the death or dying process, due to their own discomfort or confusion, the child will follow that model; if the adult model shows comfort as well as emotional upset, the child will follow that model. In either case, ask and talk about it. It will be good for both.

Part of that coming to terms will involve participation in our particular cultural/religious activities surrounding dying and death. It is important, again, to *ask* children what their wishes are regarding hospital visitation, viewing dead bodies, or attending funerals, once an accurate explanation is made of what is happening.

An infant died and was in the Intensive Care Nursery. The mother was still in recovery and the father stood outside the door of the ICN with their four-year-old daughter, wondering what to do. The head nurse suggested we ask the child what she wanted to do, with some explanation as to what she would be seeing. We took her in with her father, she looked at the baby, touched it, looked at us, and said, "Okay." Later discussion proved the image from that experience was far less traumatic than what she thought was in there.

Finally, be careful to listen for feelings of guilt from the child. Children think they are omnipotent. When a loved one dies (or a cat, dog, or goldfish) the children may think they had something to do with it. Phrases like: "If I had been better, then Gramps would not have died," or, "If I had visited him that last day...If I had minded Dad before he left..." and the like, indicate a sense of culpability for the death.

Straightforwardly telling the child that that thought is untrue, and explaining the medical or accidental cause of the death may save the child years of self punishing behavior and diminished self worth.

2. *AIDS* When the first edition of this book was published in 1988, three million people worldwide had AIDS; now that number has tripled and is expected to increase to twenty million by the end of the decade. It is already the fifth highest cause of death in U.S. women aged 18–44 and the leading cause of death in the U.S. in the 25–44 age group, having presently killed twice the number of Americans who died in Vietnam.

Nearly everyone reading this book either knows or knows of someone who has AIDS and who will die with it. Thus it is extremely important to relate the concepts in this book to the predictable results of the AIDS epidemic. While entire volumes have been written on the peculiar details of dealing with AIDS patients, it is possible to walk through the chapters of this book with that particular disease group in mind.

The same steps and suggestions apply in Section I, *Being With The Dying*. But, in addition to the usual loneliness expressed by dying patients, AIDS patients have an additional *social* isolation caused by the negative stereotypes accompanying its transmissal, and *physical* isolation inflicted by blood and body fluid precautions necessary to protect patients and caregivers from increased exposure to infection. As friends and family members flee from, reject or agonize with their relatives and loved ones, they will need significantly more support in dealing with this particularly insidious method of dying.

Section II, *Ethics and Death*, equally relates to patients dying from AIDS or ARC (AIDS-Related Complex). We are quickly learning that it is simply not true that "only old people die," as we see scores of young persons in their twenties and thirties gradually waste away and die.

Withdrawal of artificial interventions will have to be considered as the influx of AIDS patients increases. Lack of funding, along with the current certainty of death will probably result in more and more deaths at home A complicating problem of AIDS patients, however, is that they frequently have no home to which to go to die. Often they are abandoned by friends, unwanted by family, and medically indigent. Church groups, nursing homes, hospices, and state and federal insurance pools will have to combine resources to meet the coming needs in this difficult area.

Medicare Hospice regulations have been extended to cover Medicaid in order to lower costs of terminal, palliative only care for AIDS patients. In doing so, *managed, limited* medical care may well become the norm, and set the stage for such managed care of other terminally ill patients as well. The church will have to diligently monitor the ethical implications of such care, as the slippery slope may be impossible to reclimb when it comes to determining who dies and how.

The church is already examining its own stand on AIDS. Both evangelical and liberal denominations are attempting to deal with the social and religious implications of the disease. Variations on the slogans in Section III have developed, such as: "The AIDS epidemic is God's judgment on homosexuals and drug abusers"; and "God-fearing Christians need have no fear of AIDS." But we know that over a fifth of AIDS patients are between the ages of 21–28 (meaning that they had to have been infected when adolescents), and that 11 percent are women (except in the 13–19 age group where the male-female ratio is nearly 50–50). Thus as the number of heterosexual AIDS patients increases, these slogans will take their place beside the equally erroneous ones listed in Chapter 7.

Probably the greatest impact of the AIDS dilemma is to be reflected in Section IV. *Sex After Death* takes on whole new fears and anxieties. The survivor seeking intimacy must now realize that having sex with a partner is not just having sex with *that* partner, it is having sex with *all* of the people *both* partners have ever had sex with. Proper precautions are, of course, in order, including medical testing (though one would have to be retested nearly every six weeks to maintain certainty) and a new interest in celibacy.

The *Guidelines...* chapter must also now take AIDS into consideration by encouraging "safe sex," and warning of the extreme dangers of promiscuity or even serial monogamy. In every case there are no easy answers, and survivors must deal with the threat of their own death in seeking intimacy and sexual behavior after their loved one has died.

Finally, the suggestions in the "Surviving Death" chapter still apply. But, in addition, special care and consideration must be afforded those families and loved ones surviving AIDS deaths. Their increased social isolation, fed by unwarranted myths about AIDS and how it is and is not contracted and spread, is an additional dimension which will only serve to exacerbate their grief responses.

It is interesting that the AIDS crisis, for all its horror and danger, may be the precipitating factor in demanding that our culture—and our church—come to terms with the reality of death. It may, in addition, alter our sexual mores, entirely restructure our system of healthcare delivery, and force us to examine our theology of illness, death, judgment, and reconciliation.

3. Long-term response   A final item that needs exploration is that of the long term response to death. What is it like to have had a loved one die twenty years ago? How does one think of that person twenty hears hence? What feelings arise as long distances of time pass? Since most of my experience is with immediate death and bereavement, I have little information about the effects of death many years later.

Several possibilities, however, come to mind. The survivor may choose never to work through the tasks of grieving, deciding to continue life with the loved one always present in mind and thought, never reengaging in social activities to any significant level and never allowing for deep personal joy again.

It is also possible for the tasks of grieving to be adequately "worked through." The survivor may indeed go on with life with the loved one as a more and more distant and pleasant memory. Current activities could take the place of the former relationship and, from time to time, bittersweet remembrances would occur.

But it is most likely that survivors will handle bereavement the same way they handled other long term losses—childhood, adolescence, major illness, divorce, separation from family, or job change—bringing to bear the same coping skills that were helpful in other situations. Other options are possible, I am sure; I just don't yet have the data to describe them. I would be glad to hear from readers who can offer their experience about this matter.

If you have read this far, you have begun the most difficult part of the process. You have begun to face your own feelings and thoughts about death in general, and about your own personal death. You will now be better able to be of real help to others who are dying. You will also be more willing to talk with your family and loved ones about your own plans and wishes.

Indeed, like the patients and families who provided the material for this book, you have begun your own journey toward surviving death.

APPENDICES

Directive to Physicians

(The following Directive to Physicians is legal in Texas. It is meant only as a sample illustration for interested readers. Following the Cruzan decision, different states may have different restrictions. For the specific format required for a particular state, check with the State Medical Association, or see the "Handbook of Living Wills—1987 Edition" available from The Society for the Right to Die, 250 West 57th Street, New York, New York 10107.)

Directive made this_____ day _____(month, year). I _____, being of sound mind, willfully, and voluntarily make known my desire that my life shall not be artificially prolonged under the circumstances set forth below, and do hereby declare:

1. If at any time I should have an incurable or irreversible condition caused by injury, disease, or illness certified to be a terminal condition by two physicians, and where the application of life-sustaining procedures would serve only to artificially prolong the moment of my death and where my attending physician determines that my death is imminent or will result within a relatively short time without application of life-sustaining procedures, I direct that such procedures be withheld or withdrawn, and that I be permitted to die naturally.

2. In the absence of my ability to give directions regarding the use of such life-sustaining procedures, it is my intention that this directive shall be honored by my family and physicians as the final expression of my legal right to refuse medical or surgical treatment and accept the consequences from such refusal.

3. If I have been diagnosed as pregnant and that diagnosis is known to my physician, this directive shall have no force or effect during the course of my pregnancy.

4. This directive shall be in effect until it is revoked.

5. I understand the full import of this directive and I am emotionally and mentally competent to make this directive.

6. I understand that I may revoke this directive at any time.

7. I understand that Texas law allows me to designate another person to make a treatment decision for me if I should become comatose, incompetent, or otherwise mentally or physically incapable of communication. I hereby designate ——————————————— , who resides at ————————————————— to make such a treatment decision for me if I should become incapable of communicating with my physician.

If the person I have named above is unable to act on my behalf, I authorize the following person to do so:

Name ————————————————————————————

Address ———————————————————————————

I have discussed my wishes with these persons and trust their judgment.

8. I understand that if I become incapable of communication, my physician will comply with this directive unless I have designated another person to make a treatment decision for me, or unless my physician believes this directive no longer reflects my wishes.

Signed———————————————————————————

———————————————————————————————
City, County and State of Residence

(Two witnesses must sign the directive in the spaces provided below.

I am not related to the declarant by blood or marriage, nor am I the attending physician of declarant or an employee of the attending physician; or am I a patient in the healthcare facility in which the declarant is a patient, or any person who has a claim against any portion of the estate of the declarant upon his/her decease. Furthermore, if I am an employee of a healthcare facility in which the declarant is a patient, I am not involved in providing direct patient care to the declarant, nor am I directly involved in the financial affairs of the health facility.

Witness: ——————————————————————————

Witness:——————————————————————————

Durable Power of Attorney for Healthcare

Designation of Healthcare Agent

I, (insert your name)_____ appoint:
Name: _____
Address:_____
_____ Phone: _____
as my agent to make any and all healthcare decisions for me, except to the extent I state otherwise in this document. This durable power of attorney for healthcare takes effect if I become unable to make my own healthcare decisions and this fact is certified in writing by my physician.

Limitations on the decision making authority of my agent are as follows:_____

Designation of Alternate Agent
(You are not required to designate an alternate agent but you may do so. An alternate agent may make the same healthcare decisions as the designated agent if the designated agent is unable or unwilling to act as your agent. If the agent designated is your spouse, the designation is automatically revoked by law if your marriage is dissolved.)

If the person designated as my agent is unable or unwilling to make healthcare decisions for me, I designate the following persons to serve as my agent to make healthcare decisions for me as authorized by this document, who serve in the following order:

A. First Alternate Agent: Name_____
Address:_____
_____ Phone: _____

B. Second Alternate Agent: Name _____
Address:_____
_____ Phone: _____

The original of this document is kept at:_____

The following individuals or institutions have signed copies:
Name:_____
Address:_____

Name: _____
Address: _____

Duration
I understand that this power of attorney exists indefinitely from the date I execute this document unless I establish a shorter time or revoke the power of attorney. If I am unable to make healthcare decisions for myself when this power of attorney expires, the authority I have granted my agent continues to exist until the time I become able to make healthcare decisions for myself.

(IF APPLICABLE) The power of attorney ends on the following date:_____

Prior Designations Revoked
I revoke any prior durable power of attorney for healthcare.

Acknowledgment of Disclosure Statement
I have been provided with a disclosure statement explaining the effect of this document. I have read and understand that information contained in the disclosure statement.

(You must date and sign this power of attorney.)
I sign my name to this durable power of attorney for healthcare on_____ day of _____ 19___ at _____
                              City and State _____
                              (Signature) _____
                              (Print Name)_____

Statement of Witness
I declare under penalty of perjury that the principal has identified himself or herself to me, that the principal signed or acknowledged

this durable power of attorney in my presence, that I believe the principal is aware of the nature of the document and is signing it voluntarily and free from duress, that the principal requested that I serve as witness to the principal's execution of this document, and that I am not a provider of health or residential care, the operator of a community care facility, or an employee of an operator of a healthcare facility.

I declare that I am not related to the principal by blood, marriage, or adoption and that to the best of my knowledge I am not entitled to any part of the estate of the principal on the death of the principal under a will or by operation of law.

Witness Signature: _____

Print Name: _____ Date: _____

Address: _____

_____

Witness Signature: _____

Print Name: _____ Date: _____

Address: _____

_____

Home Death

(The following information has been prepared for patients and families by The St. David's Hospital Oncology Center.)

Death at home rather than in the hospital is an option that more patients and their families are beginning to consider. Because of familiar surroundings, the easier accessibility of friends, and the comfort of home rather than hospital sounds, smells, and tastes, many persons wish to die in that setting.

Although not always possible, given the extent of physical disability, the need for full time care, or the problem of severe pain control, often the same things offered in the hospital can quite easily be provided at home.

Hospital beds, bedside commodes, tray tables, and other items can be supplied by the local branch of the American Cancer Society (or other community organization), usually at no charge. Families can learn to give medications and injections; they can be taught to give bed baths and flush catheters. Special medications or appliances, i.v.'s and physical therapy all can be handled through the hospital or local home health agency.

Nurses, with a physician order, can visit several times a week as needed at home and sitters can be hired through these same agencies. If you are interested in exploring this option, the hospital or Hospice staff will work with you and your physician to make whatever arrangements are necessary.

Once home, family members often want to know what to expect when the patient is nearing death. The usual indications are:
1. *Changing breathing patterns*
   - apnea (periods of forgetting to breathe)
   - secretions accumulating in throat or lungs
   - loud bubbling sounds in lungs ("Death Rattle")
   - like snoring, these breathing sounds may be alarming to visitors, but are seldom painful to the patient

2. *Change in temperature and color*
   - bluish discoloration in feet and hands
   - extremities begin to cool, moving up legs to upper body
3. *Change in pulse*
   - increased pulse rate
   - decreased blood pressure
4. *Loss of bowel and bladder control*
5. *Decreased urinary output*
6. *Decreased responsiveness*
   - gradual withdrawal
   - difficulty swallowing
   - unable to talk, move muscles, follow with eyes
7. *Possible uncontrolled movements*
   - twitching
   - tossing and turning
   - picking at bedclothes

At the time of death you may expect the following:
1. *No breathing.*
2. *No pulse.*
3. *Change in color, usually to a dusky blue color.*
4. *Body becomes cool or cold.*
5. *May have "carbon dioxide" breathing and tighten jaw or gasp for breath a few times following loss of pulse and cessation of breathing.*
6. *Loss of facial muscle control (jaws sag, eyes may remain open).*
7. *Loss of bowel and bladder control (not always).*
8. *Possible muscle twitches.*

If you have questions or concerns about any of these issues, call the hospital oncology unit nurse, the Hospice office, your Hospice volunteer, or the Home Health after hours number for assistance at any time.

A Gift for the Dying

by
Jean Loving
Hospice Volunteer

I help dying people. And I help those they love and who love them. I am a hospice volunteer.

Becoming involved with a hospice organization had been my hope for many years. Because of frequent relocation, sometimes to cities with no active hospice, it was an impossibility until my move to Austin, Texas, in 1981. The dream was born many years ago, when, as a practicing professional nurse, I recognized that in our ongoing pursuit of the cure of disease, the needs of the dying person were sadly neglected. I was frustrated by our dehumanization of death as we denied knowledge of its nearness, or of its very possibility. After Elisabeth Kübler-Ross publicized her studies and philosophy about the needs of dying people, I began incorporating her ideas as I taught the practice of nursing. I have been committed to the concept of hospice care since that time.

In September 1982, I participated in the educational program for volunteers offered by the Austin Comprehensive Hospice Program. Experiencing the hospice philosophy has become a way of life for me, a gift beyond measure from the dying, to the dying, and for the dying.

To be a hospice volunteer, one must be able to face his or her own mortality, to view death as another stage of life, and to appreciate the value of the gift of living. There must be a willingness to be vulnerable so that those whose time to live is limited may feel comfortable, confident, and free to be unguarded as well. Hospice volunteering is an "activity of the heart," a desire to be a companion and a helper to those in the last days of their journey through life, and to those loved ones who grieve their loss. It is an exceptional way in which an individual can express a deep personal belief in the value of human existence.

An understanding of the activities of a hospice volunteer must be based on an acceptance of how each person faces his or her own impending death. Life *and* death have infinite variety; there are few generalities and no "norms." There is no right or wrong way to think, feel, and act, and there are no rules or checklists. There are far more differences than similarities. In my experience, perhaps the only guide is that people usually face death and die the way they have lived. Their reactions, behavior and outlook are the same as in the earlier stages of their lives when facing a desperate situation. Only rarely do dramatic deathbed changes occur.

Specific fears and levels of grief, anger, and acceptance are as unique as each individual. Fears are varied but sometimes are centered, not on death itself or on the unknown, but on the process of dying: Will they be alone? Will there be pain or air hunger? Will they be conscious? Many grieve for what and who they shall leave behind and for the loss of the years ahead. Some regret words left unsaid and deeds undone, and others have lived only in the past or the future, "putting in time" waiting for a better tomorrow that now will never come. I often hear, "But I still have so much to do." One lovely lady who had often put her own goals and desires behind those of her husband and children asked, "But when will I ever get my turn now?"

Some people are enraged at the injustice of dying and at life's unfairness. They wonder why it has to be happening to them and one patient was even bold enough to name who it should have been happening to instead. Their indignant rage and their struggle toward understanding often interfere with the quality of their remaining days.

Many never lose their sense of humor and often find joy in the smiles they provoke or the laughs they share with others. One stately gentleman had this retort when I introduced myself as a hospice volunteer: "Oh, you're the one who is supposed to make me happy about dying!" Another lady said, "The doctor gave me six months to live and I've made my plans so it better not be a minute more!"

Certain individuals show a calm acceptance, maintaining a dignity of the human spirit even as they experience physical losses and psychological torment, and face their final goodbyes. There are those who are spiritually peaceful and who express their belief, in actions and words, that in joy and sorrow alike, life is God given and precious no matter how limited. Some reach out to others with increasing sensitivity, adding dimensions of love and meaning to their remaining time.

The reaction of others when they discover my involvement with dying people is at times comical. In our supposedly sophisticated society, nothing can stop a conversation or cause a shift of discomfort as quickly as the mention of death. Having passed the boundary of surprise and shock, many ask the question, "But what exactly do you do?" Because we are so task oriented (we want to *do*, not just be), the answer is difficult to express. It cannot be summed up in one sentence, explained in an hour, or found in a reference book.

As a volunteer, I care. I can't take away the anguish nor understand the depth of the despair of dying persons or the grief of their loved ones, but I *care* that they hurt. I offer my help instead of an attempt to save. I'm there, not to lead, but to share, always with an awareness that it is a privilege to be allowed within the intimacy of the precious last months, weeks, days or moments of life.

I'm a friend. And yet volunteers are more than friends because they do not judge. Unlike friends, they expect and demand nothing from the relationship, they need not be protected from the ugliness of physical suffering, from expressions of emotional despair, or from the torment of lost faith. Volunteers don't try to take away the hurt or try to answer, "Why me?" They give no unsolicited advice, use no meaningless slogans, and they never discount what a person is feeling or experiencing.

Hospice volunteers never function without the support and encouragement of others. As a member of the hospice team, they share knowledge and ideas with the physician, the hospice nurse, the social worker and the pastoral counselor. Team members are committed to providing support to the patient and family at home, in one of the participating hospitals in Austin, or in local nursing homes. In addition, volunteers receive reassurance and guidance from a support system which includes other volunteers and the volunteer coordinator.

I often feel my most important function as a volunteer is listening, an *activity* that hears not only words but unexpressed feelings and meanings. I have learned to be comfortable with silence. Words cannot always be formed by someone trying to cope and make sense of it all. But shared silence can be consoling. I recall a past patient, a very proud and private person, with whom I enjoyed a close relationship. On the day she heard from her physician that her disease had advanced beyond further treatment or medicine and that her life expectancy was short, we sat together, holding hands, silent and alone. When I left, she thanked me tearfully and said, "I'm better now." Her words about death and her grief and my expressions of comfort were unspoken, yet there was intimate communication between us.

The spoken words I hear are statements of bitterness, of denial, and of anger against God, physicians, family, and sometimes themselves. On rare occasions, patients become angry at the volunteer, as when one patient asked my age and calculated just how many years I had left to live. I hear the guilts of the past, the anguish of the present, and the regret of leaving things unfinished. I also hear expressions of peace, acceptance, profound and unrelenting faith, and poignant and moving episodes from lifetimes filled with love and sharing. Sometimes the words I hear are spoken just to comfort and encourage me.

By nature I am a "toucher," and many patients welcome this form of communication, though I am careful to respect the feelings of those who might consider it an invasion of their space of privacy. People who are ill feel unlovable and unattractive at times, and a hug can be almost therapeutic as well as a demonstration of my concern. A very special patient, a lovely and gracious lady, always greeted me with outstretched arms asking for her hug of the day, a hug I often needed as well. Another patient whose sight was affected by her disease and by medication would ask as she felt me take her hand, "It's you, Jean, isn't it?" My touch, heart to heart and hand to hand, was a familiar and welcome part of her darkening days.

Touch is especially important in the last hours and moments of life since it is one of the last senses to be lost. It has been my privilege to remain with a number of patients at these times, holding hands, rubbing arms, and stroking foreheads. One patient, whose neurological disease caused numbness in her feet, welcomed a gentle massage of her feet and legs as her illness progressed. During her last moments, she had only the strength to nod yes and smile weakly as I was there to rub her feet for the last time.

As life ebbs from their bodies, speaking to patients is important even if their state of consciousness is questionable. I tell them they are not alone and indicate which of their friends and family members are present. I frequently assure them that they are loved and how much they will be missed. I vividly recall a sweet lady, apparently comatose for hours, who reacted with movements of limbs and eyes when I told her that her only daughter and grandchildren had arrived from their distant home. A sound of pleasure escaped her lips, and she died peacefully a short time later in the loving arms of her husband and daughter.

As a volunteer, I am committed to preserving and enhancing the quality of life of hospice patients, whatever time span that encompasses. I become involved in many activities: arranging and observing heartwarming reunions, smuggling a pet dog into a hospital room, participating in a bedside communion service for a family of sixteen, or helping with a manicure and makeup session for a patient.

Sometimes, and often, it is just having fun together. It's not whispering or tiptoeing around, but telling outrageous jokes and having a good belly laugh. It's arranging (with the physician's approval) for a bottle of favorite wine *and* a crystal glass to be available in a hospital room. It's going for a drive, shopping for a gown or wig, going to a movie. It's shampooing hair or shaving a neglected beard, baking favorite cookies, or hunting down the special mints which are the only things that taste really good. It's going out for a roast beef sandwich or for tacos for the patient who hasn't eaten in days, or arranging for the hospital cook to make old-fashioned chicken and dumplings.

Sometimes it means assisting with funeral plans or arranging for a last family picture to be made. Often it involves making a list of personal treasures and to whom they will be left. It may be providing a journal and encouraging the written expression of feelings too difficult to voice, or helping with letters and tape recordings which will become legacies for those left behind. It's making arrangements for a party or for little gifts to be handmade, perhaps painted bookmarks for each grandchild, or a knitted cap to be completed and remembered with. It's making birthdays and anniversaries special, and having a joyful Christmas celebration even in a hospital room. Little acts of kindness and pleasures of the moment cannot be substitutes for good health and long life, but when moments are few, they really matter.

Families of dying people often feel isolated and afraid, and helping them cope can mean that the patient is surrounded with gentle, loving, and unafraid loved ones. One family was tired and grieving, yet diligent in keeping a loved one at the bedside at all times. At one point, the sole attendant was a loving 21-year-old granddaughter. When I entered the room, she was obviously distressed and afraid, expressing her fear of being along with her grandmother and of how death would occur. Gently I told her that I thought it would be a quiet and peaceful end, just "like a clock running down." Later we cried together and she thanked me for easing her fear and said, "It was just like you said it would be."

In other ways families can be assisted by arranging the delivery of equipment needed at home, helping with endless forms and papers, providing a break for the primary caregiver or transportation to physician's offices or treatment centers, and being a liaison between the family and the hospice team. Sometimes it is simply providing the encouragement and the opportunity to have a good cry.

Why am I a hospice volunteer? What's in it for me? Without question it keeps my priorities in order, reminding me of what is important in life and what isn't and of how precious a gift each day is. I have discovered inner resources of mind and spirit and a reserve of empathy which had been unknown and previously unused.

Many times my memories are my rewards, because as I give part of myself to others, parts of them remain within me, continuing to teach me about the wonders of the human spirit. And there can be little more satisfying than to hear, "I couldn't make it without you," or "You are the *only* one I can tell how I really feel." It is payment beyond measure to see the drawn face of a grieving spouse light up as I rush back to the bedside of his dying wife, and to hear a patient when readmitted to the hospital ask, not for his physician or for a special nurse, but for me.

Hospice Austin has brought many blessings to my life besides the warm experiences with patients. I have the association of people who are stimulating, supportive, and committed, and I have made special friendships that are and will be a meaningful part of my life. I have a deeper understanding of myself, I treasure my relationships with others more, and I more fully appreciate the value of time. Perhaps the real reward is that I feel that what I am doing really makes a difference.

There are times when I become depressed. I am sad when I fail to establish a relationship with someone in need, and I grieve when death separates me from a special patient. Sometimes I am angry because I've been left behind and will miss the precious opportunities to learn and grow that patients give me. As a dear friend and fellow volunteer expressed it, "If you weren't doing a good job, it wouldn't hurt."

I get my strength and my comfort from my faith in God, my belief in what I am trying to do, and through the support of the hospice team, my family, and friends. I still must strive to keep a balance in my life, often reminding myself that I'm not the *only* one who can help. Periodic breaks allow me to "refill my cup" and replenish my emotional reserves.

As a hospice volunteer, I see grief, pain, injustice, and sad goodbyes. I also see love, caring, goodness, and the miracles of human understanding. And most often, after the special gift of helping someone I care about die with dignity, with the peace of acceptance and surrounded by loved ones, having had the opportunity to say his or her goodbyes, I am eager and impatient to be allowed the privilege to do it again.

Resources

Becker, Ernest. *The Denial of Death*. New York: The Free Press, 1973.

Bugen, Lawrence. *Death and Dying: Theory, Research and Practice*. Dubuque, Iowa: William C. Brown Publishers, 1979.

Callahan, Daniel. *Setting Limits: Medical Goals in an Aging Society*. New York: Simon and Schuster, 1987.

Englehardt, Jr., Tristram. *The Foundations of Bioethics*. New York: Oxford University Press, 1986.

Ford, J. Massyngbaerde. *The Silver Lining: Personalized Scriptural Wake Services*. Mystic, Connecticut: Twenty-Third Publications, 1987.

_____, *Welcoming Heaven: Prayers and Reflections for the Dying and Those Who Love Them*. Mystic, Connecticut: Twenty-Third Publications, 1990.

Kopp, Sheldon, and Claire Flanders. *What Took You So Long?* Science and Behavior Books, 1979.

Meyer, Charles. *God's Laughter and Other Heresies*. Austin (7507 Stonecliff Circle, Austin, Texas 78731), 1990.

Morgan, Ernest. *A Manual of Death Education and Simple Burial*. Burnsville, North Carolina: Celo Press, 1980.

Parkes, Colin Murray. *Studies of Grief in Adult Life*. Tavistock Publications, 1972.

Shelp, Earl E., and Ronald H. Sunderland. *AIDS and the Church*. Philadelphia: The Westminister Press, 1987.

Slaikeu, Karl. *Crisis Intervention: A Handbook for Practice and Research*. Boston: Allyn and Bacon, 1983.

Slaikeu, Karl, and Steve Lawhead. *Up From The Ashes: How to Survive and Grow Through Personal Crisis*. Grand Rapids, Michigan: Zondervan Publishing House, 1987.

Timmerman, Joan. *The Mardi Gras Syndrome: Rethinking Christian Sexuality*. New York: The Crossroad Publishing Company, 1984.

Weatherhead, Leslie. *The Will of God*. Nashville: Abingdon-Cokesbury Books, 1944.

Widowed Persons Service
AARP, 1909 K Street, N.W.
Washington, D.C. 20049

National Hospice Office
Suite 307
1901 North Fort Meyer Drive
Arlington VA 22209

The Living Bank
P.O. Box 6725
Houston TX 77265

"As Long as There Is Life" (film)
The Hospice Institute
765 Prospect Street
New Haven CT 06511

Society for the Right to Die
250 West 57th Street
New York NY 10107